P9-BYD-053

Writing this book has been a painful experience for me. Remembering all the family, friends, and leaders I knew who were murdered by the Khomeini regime was devastating. But I had no choice.

These brutal thugs and savages destroyed millions of Iranian lives, and I cannot sit silently while I see them getting ready to do the same thing to my country, the United States. This book is intended not just as a picture of where we are but a wakeup call, to let Americans know that the Khomeini network of fascist mullahs is actively planning to destroy us.

The threat is very real, and when they have nuclear weapons, it will be almost impossible to get rid of them. The time to act is now, and we must act together with the Iranian people themselves. They will fight to establish a secular democracy if we give them the things they need to get the job done. They wanted democracy in 1906, and they want it today. They cannot get it by themselves, and nobody but the United States can help them get it.

Many westerners look at the situation and say we must take Iran's nuclear weapons away from the mullahs. In reality it is easier and more practical to take the country away from them instead. A democratic secular Iran can be trusted with nuclear weapons just as much as the nearby countries that already have them: Russia, Pakistan, India, China, and Israel. We are not used to thinking this way, but a strong, democratic pro-American Iran would be a tremendously effective weapon in the war against terrorism. Terrorists cannot be trusted with nuclear weapons of any kind; with such weapons, they threaten not only the United States but all governments and civilizations on the planet.

A NATION UNDER SIEGE

Nukes, Mullahs, and the
Ultimate Nightmare

M. Blake

DS
318.825
B6
2005

60791783   5-4-06

c, 1

A NATION UNDER SIEGE
Nukes, Mullahs, and the Ultimate Nightmare
Copyright © 2005 by M. Blake

All rights reserved. No part of this book may be reproduced or transmitted in any form or by any means, electronic, mechanical, or photographic, by recording or any information storage or retrieval system now known or to be invented or adapted, without prior permission obtained in writing from the publisher, except for a reviewer quoting brief passages in a review written for inclusion in a journal, magazine, newspaper, or broadcast.

Requests to reproduce should be directed to the publisher at blakepress@yahoo.com

First Edition.

ISBN Number 0-9764155-0-X

Library of Congress Catalog Number to be assigned.

Blake Press
San Francisco, California

04 05 06 07 08 09 10 10 9 8 7 6 5 4 3 2 1

PRINTED IN THE UNITED STATES OF AMERICA

Dedication

I dedicate this book to my dear brother, who fought for freedom and democracy and was tortured and murdered at the hands of Iran's criminal mullahs.

This book is also dedicated to:

the members of America's armed forces, and especially the brave Marines, who are fighting for freedom and risking their lives to better the lives of others

the brave CIA officer Mike Spann, who died fighting for democracy in Afghanistan

the 241 brave U. S. Marines who were killed in the 1983 bombing attack in Lebanon, which was carried out by local terrorists trained and financed by the Iranian government

Lieutenant Colonel and CIA Station Chief William F. Buckley and Lieutenant Colonel William Higgins, who were kidnaped, tortured, and killed by agents financed and directed by the Iranian government

the brave Iranian generals of 1979, who refused to bow to the mullahs or renounce democracy and freedom. They walked proudly to their deaths, killed by men who could never hope to be their moral equals

Mohammed Reza Shah Pahlavi who, dying of cancer, left his beloved Iran with tears in his eyes, hoping to save the lives of thousands of Iranians and prevent millions from shedding their blood

Prime Minister Shahpour Bakhtiar, who stood up for democracy and against Khomeini and who was murdered in Paris by Iranian terrorist assassins.

Table of Contents

Prologue

It was the fourth Tuesday in January, and my eyes were glued to the TV screen. President Bush was delivering his State of the Union address for 2002, and the words rang true. After years of doubt and uncertainty, America's leaders were openly admitting that terrorism is a serious threat to life, love, and the future of the human race.

"We have seen the depth of our enemies' hatred in videos where they laugh about the loss of innocent life. And the depth of their hatred is equaled by the madness of the destruction they design. We have found diagrams of American nuclear power plants and public water facilities, detailed instructions for making chemical weapons, surveillance maps of American cities and thorough descriptions of landmarks in America and throughout the world. . . . Thousands of dangerous killers, schooled in the methods of murder, often supported by outlaw regimes, are now spread throughout the world like ticking time bombs set to go off without warning."

As an American raised in Iran, I knew how much of this tide of evil and destruction came from there. It made me cry to think how far Iran had fallen morally and spiritually in less than twenty-five years. It was not like that before . . .

Iran in the '60s was a magical place. Those years were filled with peace, prosperity, and optimism. Cars moved along wide, uncrowded city streets, lined with tall trees. Crime was low, and almost everybody had food to eat, a place to live, and clothing to wear. There was still poverty in some rural villages, but many villagers were becoming homeowners, for the first time in thousands of years. The British and

Russian occupation forces were gone, and Iran was moving rapidly into a bright new future. And everyone loved Americans.

An American visitor could go almost anywhere and be invited in for tea or dinner with an Iranian family. We were fascinated by these people and eager to learn more about them. Our country's leader, Shah Reza II (Pahlavi), encouraged us to befriend Americans and learn to dream big dreams, just like they did. And he led us by his personal example.

The Shah was a friend and ally to America for more than thirty years. His friendship with President Kennedy was legendary, and the First Lady, Jacqueline Kennedy, was widely revered and loved throughout Iran.

We were devastated by the Kennedy assassination in 1963. Adults and children wept openly, and in Iranian schools children wrote poems and songs honoring the memory of President Kennedy. We felt as if one of our own family had died. He wanted Iran to succeed and prosper, just as we did.

The Shah was firmly pro-American, even when it was not popular with Iran's neighbors. He also insisted on religious tolerance, creating a climate in which Moslems, Jews, Christians, Zoroastrians, Bahais, Buddhists, and others were able to practice their religions freely without fear of going to jail. We Americans tend to take religious freedom and tolerance for granted because we have had it for centuries, ever since the founding of Rhode Island by Roger Williams and Pennsylvania by William Penn. But in Iran such freedoms have been an on-again, off-again sort of thing.

The Shah ruled for thirty-eight years, longer than any other Iranian ruler of the twentieth century. He pushed Iran into an aggressive modernization program and carefully nurtured the growth of the blue collar and white collar middle classes. The pace of growth and change was exhilarating for young adults like myself, disturbing for middle-aged Iranians, and terrifying for the elderly and those who had grown wealthy under the medieval way of doing things.

In the 1970s the Shah came under attack from an incurable form of cancer. The Iranian body politic came under attack from another form of cancer in the person of Ayatollah Ruhollah Khomeini. As the Shah grew weaker, Khomeini grew stronger. It seemed as if the entire country fell under an evil spell. Hundreds of thousands of educated, highly intelligent Iranians came to believe that Khomeini was the friend of morality, freedom, and prosperity, and that the Shah was the enemy of such things. This was the opposite of the truth.

As the educated people added their support to the illiterate villagers who already supported Khomeini, millions of other Iranians came to support him as well. A consensus emerged that no post-Shah government could succeed without Khomeini's endorsement. Once Khomeini was seen as indispensable, the success of the Khomeini outlaw regime was assured.

The Shah left Iran in January of 1979, and Khomeini returned to Iran the next month. He took power and retained it until he died in 1989. His successor, Ayatollah Khamenei, has held power ever since.

In the Khomeini outlaw regime, the ultimate decision-maker is the Vale-e-Faqih, which is best translated into English as the Supreme Leader. This is a lifetime position, and Khomeini held it until his death in 1989. He originally chose Ayatollah Montazeri as his successor, but in 1988 Montazeri criticized the slaughter of more than 8,000 prisoners. This annoyed Khomeini, so the position went to Khamenei instead. Khamenei was a hojatolislam, the second highest grade of cleric, so they promoted him to ayatollah to meet the threshold requirements for Supreme Leader. This did not make Khamenei the number one ayatollah in Iran, however. The relative rank of different ayatollahs is not determined by a formal system but rather is based on the level of respect and prestige they have among each other and with the general Islamic public. The Supreme Leader should, in theory, be chosen from among the ranks of the greatest and most respected ayatollahs. Khamenei was essentially a rookie ayatollah promoted over the heads of many senior ayatollahs.

After becoming the Supreme Leader, Khamenei tried to get all the ayatollahs senior to him in prestige to agree that he was the number one ayatollah of the age. This would have made his fatwas (decrees) as binding and irrevocable as Khomeini's. Several of the most important ayatollahs have refused to do this, because they view Khamenei as inferior to themselves.

After eight years of watching Khamenei issue preposterous opinions on religious matters, Ayatollah Montazeri went even further. In November of 1997, he openly stated that Khamenei was not competent to issue religious rulings. He was promptly put under house arrest and forbidden from making speeches or other public activities. The house arrest was not lifted until 2003, by which time he was eighty-one years old and in poor health. Khomeini and his followers turned Iran into what it is today: a key member of the "Axis of Evil".

The three countries in the Axis of Evil stretched out like a chain, with a missing link where China is. After the defeat of the Taliban government in Afghanistan, Iraq, Iran, and North Korea earned the Axis of Evil name by becoming the top three countries for supporting terrorists. They were sincerely dedicated to the destruction of America and all other countries with governments chosen by the people. They were equally dedicated to the destruction of all Western civilization. Even countries with Islamic governments were on their hit list.

Only one of the three countries has enough resources to actually do it, and that is Iran. North Korea is bankrupt and unable to feed its people. Iraq has elected new leaders and is moving away from terrorism. Iraq is struggling to build a democratic government that can stand up to terrorist atrocities, foreign subversion, and the constant attempts to break it into smaller countries that would discriminate on the basis of race, religion, or regional prejudice.

But Iran is different. Its population is young and healthy, it has abundant natural resources, and it has money. Some of this money has been spent in Europe, causing several European countries and industries to become dependent on Iran for their prosperity. France, for example, could not boycott Iran without losing two billion euros a year in sales.

But more importantly, the Iranian government will have stockpiles of nuclear weapons in less than five years. Once these weapons of mass destruction are on hand, the cost of invading Iran will become too steep for most governments to risk.

America has avoided this problem so far. America's economy is not dependent on Iran, due to the trade embargo imposed by the United States in 1979.

In addition, America is too far away for Iran's missiles to reach. By contrast, American missiles based in Iraq or Afghanistan could reach most Iranian targets if there were an open outbreak of hostilities.

America's armed forces are stronger and better trained than Iran's. The Iranian armed forces were unable to defeat Saddam Hussein after eight years of fighting, whereas the Americans removed him from power in less than a month.

The Iranian government concluded that it was too dangerous to engage in direct military combat with the United States. Instead, they turned to terrorism, using their oil income to hire terrorists from other countries to carry out their dirty work. Most terrorist attacks have used conventional explosives, but the Iranian government would prefer to equip its terrorists with nuclear weapons.

The majority of Iranians do not want to go down this path. They do not hate everybody who is not a Moslem and do not want to destroy them. Many of them want democracy and freedom to dress as they please, go where they want, say what they want, and have any friends they want. This is particularly true for Iranians under thirty, who comprise a majority of the population.

The purpose of this book is to convince you that America has a window of opportunity in Iran. Khomeini's people had twenty-five years to show what they could do, and they did evil rather than good. Iran is poorer today than it was under the Shah, the people have no rights, and they are tired of it. They want an elected democratic government, and they want to get rid of their current rulers, the Khomeini outlaw regime.

We have a chance to help the Iranian people replace a terrorist government with a democratic government that can restore Iran to its proper place as a modern nation at peace with the world. The Iranian people want leaders who love peace, freedom, and democracy more than uranium, plutonium, and missiles.

Everyone would benefit if Iran becomes such a country. But the Iranians cannot do it alone, and the United States is the only country with the ability to help them bring this change about before the window of opportunity closes.

Chapter 1

Before the Fall

Before the 1979 revolution, Iran was an enemy of terrorists and acted quickly and decisively against them. Shah Reza II had a strong military and a good intelligence service that sought out terrorists before they did serious harm.

The shah also promoted land reform and home ownership for low income rural people. The first step was to enable them to own land. Most land outside the cities was then owned by a small number of wealthy families, while the peasants lived on the land and worked in the fields. The Shah's White Revolution compelled wealthy landowners to surrender hundreds of the villages they owned so that the peasants who lived there could own the land they worked on. This angered some of the land owners and clerics, but it improved life for millions of people until the Khomeini Revolution in 1979. Khomeini's people turned the clock back 1300 years for people in the countryside, who are now worse off than before.

In the early 1970s, the shah declared that the Middle East should be free of nuclear weapons and pledged that under his leadership Iran would never develop them. He kept his word, and while he ruled the country there was no development of nuclear weapons.. Today, Iran's secret nuclear weapons program is much further along than the UN and most other observers thought it was. The first nuclear bombs may be ready in 2005, and soon Iran will have missiles that can deliver nuclear warheads to Western Europe, Alaska, and Canada.

Carter and the Shah at the twilight of his reign

How did Iran change so quickly from a peaceful, growing country to an outlaw nation that has its neighbors worried?

Several forces combined to cause the disaster. First of all, the shah fell ill with cancer. When he left Iran in January of 1979, his eyes were full of tears. He was already terminally ill, and he could not bear to think of what might happen to his people after he was gone. He died in Cairo on July 27, 1980.

A second factor was the shah's disdain for violence and killing. He had the best armed forces in the region, and an excellent intelligence service, but he could not bear to shed the blood of Iranians, even those who wanted to destroy the country and slaughter millions of people. The Iranian army had seasoned officers who could have destroyed Khomeini's forces in less than a year, but they were never ordered to do so. The shah was also unwilling to order the assassination of Khomeini while he was still in exile. The shah viewed this as uncivilized, undemocratic behavior. This is true, but the result of this forbearance was the slaughter of hundreds of thousands of Iranian citizens, an eight-year war with Iraq, and the murder of Iranian expatriates in Europe and Asia. Most of these lives would have been saved if Khomeini himself had been killed before 1979. Instead, Khomeini lived another ten years and killed hundreds of thousands, perhaps millions, of people before he finally died in 1989.

Another factor in the tragedy was the American president at the time. Jimmy Carter was one of the three worst American presidents of the twentieth century when it came to foreign affairs. He had little prior experience in dealing with other nations and cultures. He judged foreign leaders by how well their behavior matched his ideas of human rights, judged solely by the cultural standards of American colleges. He liked Marxist leaders, and he disliked kings, shahs, emperors, and conservative military dictators. He did not care what a country's prior relations with America had been; human rights were much more important to him.

The shah did not receive high marks when President Carter privately graded him. It did not matter that the shah had been a loyal ally of Presidents Eisenhower, Kennedy, Johnson, Nixon, and Ford. The shah's land reforms did not impress Carter, because the wealthy landowners did not lose everything and some of the peasants did not benefit. It is even possible that some of Carter's advisers had a grudge against the shah for the overthrow of Mossadegh in 1953.

Some of these advisers had high opinions of Khomeini at the time. Andrew Young, Carter's representative to the United Nations, called Khomeini a twentieth century saint.[1]

The shah's attempts to allow freedom of the press, after 2,500 years of kings, emperors, and censorship, actually displeased President Carter, who thought they were insincere and insufficient. The shah probably would have done better if he had imitated Fidel Castro, who legalized prostitution but banned classified ads and the freedoms of press and religion.

President Carter strongly pressured the shah not to take action against the rebel forces. Some commentators would go further and say that Carter originally supported Khomeini and wanted him to take over Iran, but little evidence of this has been found in government records from the Carter era. Similar accusations have been made against the British government, with a similar lack of documentary support.

In any event, Carter's input caused the shah to vacillate in his responses to the violence, which in turn caused many Iranians to assume that he was a coward and bully. The shah was also urged to avoid harsh criticisms of Khomeini, who was blaming the shah for everything that was wrong and many things that weren't. The shah heeded this advice, which caused many people to assume that Khomeini's criticisms had some truth to them. Carter was silent when Khomeini's forces locked 600 people inside a movie theater, burned them alive, and blamed it on the shah. No prompt denial came from the shah, and for several years many Iranians assumed that the shah was the guilty party. Perhaps some of President Carter's advisers believed the lies also.

As a result of these and other factors, Khomeini and his forces of evil conquered Iran despite having inferior fighters with poor training and equipment. The shah's army never fought them in an organized, systematic manner, even though it was better armed, better trained, and better prepared. Khomeini showed his gratitude for this by killing virtually all the top Iranian army generals at the first opportunity.

Khomeini then went on to outmaneuver President Carter in the Iranian hostage crisis, fight a useless eight-year war with Saddam Hussein, and establish Iran as the world's largest supporter and financier of terrorism.

Carter, Khomeini, and Saddam are all out of office now, but Iran continues to be the world's leading planner and banker for terrorist activities. The Iranian government is now developing nuclear weapons as quickly as possible, hoping to raise the death toll of each terrorist attack to 250,000 or more, instead of the current level of 50 to 3,000 people.

The Iranian government must be put out of business in the near future, and it must be done with the support of the Iranian people. Fortunately, the majority of Iranians hate their government with a passion, and they would be happy to replace it, if we give them the tools they need to win.

How could intelligent people like the Iranians tolerate such a terrible government? The answer begins with a look at Iran's history.

Chapter 2

Iranian History Up to World War II

Iran is a nation of about sixty-eight million people, located in Central Asia. It sits on a high plane bordered by mountains on three sides and the Persian Gulf on the fourth. Its western neighbors are the Middle Eastern countries of Iraq, Kuwait, and Turkey, while its eastern neighbors are the Central Asian countries of Turkmenistan, Afghanistan, and Pakistan. On the north, Iran is bordered by Armenia, Azerbaijan, and the Caspian Sea. To the south is nothing but water, the Persian Gulf and the Indian Ocean.

Iran's history is over 2500 years long. The most important part of that history, for us, is from the end of World War II to the present. During that time Iran changed from a relatively weak agricultural country pushed around by Britain and the Soviet Union to a much stronger industrial country with a nuclear weapons program and links to terrorist programs all over the world.

Clay figures dating back to 6,000 BC suggest that people have lived there for more than 8,000 years. They were made by the Elamites, who lived to the east of where the Tigris and Euphrates Rivers meet in Mesopotamia (modern day Iraq). Their capital was Susa, which was on the coast at that time but is now inland due to the buildup of silt from the rivers for thousands of years.

The Elamites had wood, metals, marble, and precious stones, which they traded with the Babylonians, Assyrians, and other people to the west. These other countries had abundant crops and food but not much else. The Elamites also did business with people to the east, including Afghanistan and India.

Persian culture is not derived from the Arabs or Elamites, but from a group called the Aryans, which most modern scholars believe originated in Central Asia in a region overlapping eastern Iran, Kazakhstan, Turkmenistan, and northwestern Afghanistan. Around 2000 B.C. a sizable group of Aryans left this area. One group headed southeast through Afghanistan to India, and the other group headed west, to northern Mesopotamia. Later on a third group of Aryans headed south through Afghanistan and settled in eastern Iran and Baluchistan, which is now in southwestern Pakistan.

The Aryans who headed west to Mesopotamia divided again. The northern group, known as the Medes, arrived in northern Mesopotamia and northwestern Persia around 1000 B.C. The southern group, known as the Persians, arrived in the Fars area of Iran at about the same time. The word Persia is derived from Fars, and so is Iran's national language, Farsi.

In 612 BC the Medes invaded Assyria and destroyed Nineveh, its capital. The Babylonians, who had been under Assyrian control, regained local control, rebuilt Babylon, built the Tower of Babel, conquered Jerusalem, and took the Jews back to Babylon as slaves.

The period around 600 BC was also important to Persian history because of the activities of Zoroaster[2], whose teachings formed the basis of the Zoroastrian religion. He was born about 628 BC near Tehran, in Azerbaijan, or in Balkh, Afghanistan, depending on which source one believes. This date is based on the legend that he was born 258 years before Alexander the Great conquered Persepolis (330 BC).

At age 40 (588 BC), Zoroaster converted one of the regional rulers to Zoroastrianism, and after that it grew and became the dominant religion throughout Persia. It remained that way for roughly 1200 years, until Shah Yezdigerd III was overthrown by Arab Moslems in the seventh century AD. Today the Zoroastrian religion has only a few active practitioners, most of them located in specific regions in Iran and India. Their core teaching can be described as follows:

Iran and neighboring countries.

A human being can tell the difference between good and evil and can choose between them. This is a big responsibility for oneself and others. A person is good if he or she chooses to think good thoughts, speak good words, and do good deeds. A person is evil if he or she chooses to think evil thoughts, and that person will speak evil words and do evil deeds as well. Good deeds lead you to what is good, but evil deeds keep you away from it.

The religious foundation of Iran is Zoroastrianism, not Islam. The Shi'ite branch of Islam, the current dominant religion in Iran, rests on top of that foundation. Important Iranian cultural practices, such as the springtime holiday Nourouz, are not found in other Islamic countries because they arose out of Zoroastrianism. The Khomeini regime tried unsuccessfully to eliminate Nourouz and other Zoroastrian traditions but finally gave up in the face of passive but determined resistance by the Iranian people.

Zoroastrianism is a monotheistic religion that teaches that there is a single benevolent Creator that is supreme over all beings, including tribal gods. It also teaches that there is an ongoing struggle between good, personified by Ahura Mazda (or Ormazd) and evil, personified by Ahriman (or Angra Mainyu). The struggle still has a few thousand years to go, but in the end, Ahura Mazda will win and Ahriman will lose.

Zoroastrianism focuses on the battle between good and evil in terms of personal choice. This is summarized in the phrase, "Good thoughts, good words, good actions." Zoroastrianism insists that everyone knows the difference between good and evil and can choose which kind of thoughts to think. If you say you can't tell the difference, you have chosen the Kingdom of the Lie, whether or not you admit it to yourself or others[3].

Zoroastrianism emphatically rejects the central ideas of modern nihilism that we cannot tell the difference between good and evil and that there is no real difference. It maintains that everyone can tell the difference. Shi'ite Islam largely agrees with this, but adds that if you aren't sure whether something is good or evil, discuss it with others, particularly learned people. Ayatollah Sistani of Iraq would be an example of the genuine Shi'ite tradition.

Khomeini's form of Islam, by contrast, preaches that most people are too stupid to tell the difference between good and evil and need someone to tell them. When the ayatollahs disagree, they follow what the Supreme Leader says, because the Supreme Leader is always right. Khomeini was the first Supreme Leader, of course.

Khomeinism is not really Islam, but more of a personality cult founded by a psychopath with professional training as an Islamic cleric. Islam seeks to make people smart, kind, and better servants of Allah, but Khomeinism sought to make them brutal, less intelligent, and better servants of the Supreme Leader. The Zoroastrian elements of Persian culture inoculated the people against Khomeinism, and Khomeini's attempts to abolish Zoroastrian traditions were rejected by the Moslems of Iran as well as by the Zoroastrians and members of other minority religions.

Zoroastrian farvahar carved in stone at Persepolis, the ancient Persian capital

The optimism and personal empowerment of Zoroastrianism have influenced Iranians for more than 2500 years. It has given them confidence that they know good from evil and can figure out what to do in any given situation. It has also inoculated them against the idea that they need to be ordered about like sheep. Just as many American Catholics support the Vatican but disagree with its position on abortion, so many Iranians initially supported the Khomeini government while rejecting its doctrine that they were too stupid to tell good from evil.

This view has enabled modern Iranians of the twenty-first century to form the clear and strong determination that the Khomeini regime must be replaced with a government that reflects the desires of the Iranian people. They do not want to use nuclear weapons, nerve gas, or germ warfare on anyone. They just want to lead normal lives and show the world what a free and independent Iran can achieve.

One of the tests some historians use in evaluating a religion is to look at the kind of rulers who appear after the religion has been adopted. The first great Zoroastrian ruler was Cyrus the Great, who came along roughly fifty years after Zoroastrianism caught on. He was one of the earliest rulers to treat people decently after he conquered them, and his declaration of human rights and tolerance of differences is widely respected even today.

In 550 BC Cyrus captured the capital of the Medes' kingdom, Ekbatana. Instead of destroying it, he negotiated a peace under which he ruled a combined Persian-Median empire with regional administrators from both groups.

When word of this leniency and decent treatment got out, it made a big impression on people. Conduct like this was rare in the ancient world, and it paid off. When Cyrus marched his army to Babylon eleven years later, the citizens surrendered without a fight, on the theory that he would be an improvement over their existing rulers. Cyrus surpassed their expectations. He rebuilt slum housing, protected the weak, enacted laws, built roads, and did many other things to improve their quality of life. In 536 BC he let the Jews return to Jerusalem and rebuild their temple.

In 535 BC Cyrus issued a declaration of human rights, which included the assertion that people should be tolerant of each other and their differences. This attitude was virtually unheard of in that era.

Cyrus died in 529 BC and was buried in a tomb in Pasargadae, then the capital of Persia. The tomb is still standing today. It bears an inscription stating that the flat plain all around it was once a mighty city, pointing out that all earthly matters are short-lived, and ending with the words "Do not envy me."

Cyrus's successor, Darius I, expanded the Persian kingdom until it stretched from Egypt in the west to India in the east. It was a tremendous amount of territory to rule in an age when there were no telephones and the fastest mode of transportation was by horse.

Cyrus and Darius are called the founders of the Hakhamenesh (Achaemenid) Dynasty, which lasted for about 230 years. The last of these kings was defeated by Alexander the Great in around 330 BC, and the dynasty never recovered. A group called the Seleucids took over for about 100 years, then were replaced by a non-Persian group, the Parthians, who lived near the Caspian Sea to the east of the Medes.

The Parthians ran the show for about 450 years, from about 220 BC to 224 AD. They were tough customers who got into frequent fights with the Romans and others, but generally came out all right. They were finally defeated in 224 AD by a Persian ruler, Ardeshir I from Fars. He started the Sassanid Dynasty, which lasted for about 400 years and managed to recapture a lot of the land once ruled by Cyrus and Darius I.

The Sassanid dynasty ended in 636 AD when the Arabs invaded Mesopotamia, fought a tough three-day battle, and defeated the forces of Yezdigerd III. The Arabs were at the beginning of a 600-year empire based on Islam, whereas the Persians were tired from a series of expensive and unproductive wars with the Greeks and the loss of several kings in a relatively short time.

Cyrus the Great's declaration of human rights

The Arab conquerors converted the Persians from Zoroastrianism to Islam by killing the ones who refused to become Moslems. The technique worked. Today ninety-nine percent of all Iranians are Moslems. The rest include Jews, Zoroastrians, Christians, and Bahais.

Various Arab dynasties and groups ruled Persia for the next 300 years, during which Arab culture and literature became widespread. Some Persians were appointed as regional administrators. In 900 AD one of the regional administrators, Ismail I of Bukhara, rebelled and set up his own kingdom in eastern Persia. This gave rise to the Samanid Dynasty, which sponsored a rebirth of Persian nationalism and culture.

The Samanids lasted for about 150 years, then were replaced by the Seljuq Turks. The Seljuqs ruled until 1157, then were replaced by a native Persian dynasty that ruled until 1219, when Genghis Khan's Mongol horde invaded, looting, killing, and destroying everything in its path.

Many of the Mongol invaders developed a liking for the Persian way of life. They married Persian women, had families, and settled down. The Mongol Empire splintered into local governments and remained that way until the early 1400s. At that time a Mongol operating out of Samarkand, Timur the Lame, aka Tamerlane, revived the Mongol empire and way of life. His dynasty lasted approximately a century and was replaced by the Safavid Dynasty, which lasted about 250 years.

The Safavids started off strong but lost a major battle to the Turks and had to give up a lot of territory. One of the Safavids, Abbas I, hired an English military consultant in 1599, who rebuilt the army and enabled them to win battles and regain territory. Abbas I died in 1629, but his successors were able to coast for another 100 years, until the last of them was overthrown in 1732 by one of his generals, Nader Shah.

Nader Shah is considered the founder of the Afsharid dynasty, which lasted about eighteen years. Not much of a dynasty, really, when you consider that Nader himself ruled for fifteen years (1732-1747) and the last three Afsharid kings combined ruled for less than three years (1747-1749).

There was chaos in the country from 1749 until 1757, when one of Nader Shah's generals, Karim Khan Zand, took power. He placed the infant grandson of the last Safavid ruler on the throne and proclaimed himself regent. He reformed taxes, promoted trade, built roads and buildings, and helped artists and scholars. He also gave the British a toehold in Iran by allowing the East India Company to open an office in Bushehr.

This decision was probably a net plus for Iran, because the English brought with them the concepts of democracy and limitations on the divine right of kings. As a result, the Iranian people became exposed to these ideas sooner than most of their neighbors and developed a stronger desire to try them.

Zand died in 1779, and the next five kings served a combined total of fifteen years. The last of them was defeated by a Qajari rebel, Agha Mohammad Khan, in 1794. The Qajaris were not ethnic Persians but Turkmenis living in Azerbaijan, which was then part of Persia.

Mr. Khan is considered the founder of the Qajari dynasty, but he only ruled for three years. He was assassinated in 1797 and his nephew took over. The nephew, Fath Ali Shah, ruled for thirty-seven years, but he lost a lot of territory to the Russians, including Armenia and Azerbaijan.

During this time the major European nations began taking a serious interest in Persia, with the British and the Russians leading the pack. They preferred dealing with weak and insolvent Persian rulers, but they had the military power to intimidate strong rulers as well.

After the death of Fath Ali Shah, his grandson ruled for fourteen years (1834-1848). The grandson died in 1848, and Fath Ali's son, Nasiruddin Shah, took over and ruled until 1896. He was a clever and skillful man; very few other Iranian rulers stayed in power as long as he did. He tried to play the British and Russians against each other, but both of those countries expanded their influence, despite his best efforts. The British helped set up Afghanistan and incorporated the former Persian city of Herat into it, while the Russians conquered Turkmenistan and Uzbekistan.

The Persian government found it hard to compete with late nineteenth century Europeans, and the national debt increased sharply. The Europeans eventually gained so much influence that many Persians were convinced their ruler had betrayed them.

Nasiruddin Shah was assassinated in 1896. His son Mozaffaruddin Shah then ruled until his death on January 4, 1907. He granted concessions to Europeans in return for bribes, which he spent on himself. The Persian people grew tired of this and began demanding a constitution. In July of 1906 the mullahs (clerics) organized a huge sit-down strike in Tehran. The following month the shah reluctantly signed a decree establishing a constitution and the Majlis, the Persian legislature. The elections were held in October 1906, and the Majlis started in session the same month.

The written constitution was finished by December, and Shah Mozaffaruddin signed it only a few days before his death in January 1907. The constitution provided for a bicameral legislature, separation of powers, checks and balances, and a monarch as the head of state.

Mozaffaruddin's successor to the throne was Crown Prince Muhammad Ali Mirza. He was crowned on January 19, 1907.

Muhammad Ali Shah Qajar was perhaps the most perverted, cowardly, and vice-sodden monster that had disgraced the throne of Persia in many generations. He hated and despised his subjects from the beginning of his career, and from having a notorious scoundrel for his Russian tutor, he easily became the avowed tool

The Majlis building in Tehran

and satrap of the Russian Government and its agent in Persia for
stamping out the rights of the people.[4]

Muhammad Ali[5] got into trouble with the Majlis when he tried to
borrow 400,000 pounds from the British and Russians. He decided to
hire Atabak-i-Azam (aka Aminu's- Sultan) as his Prime Minister.
Atabak had previously served as Prime Minister under Muhammad
Ali's father and grandfather. He took the oath of office in April of
1907 and began trying to persuade the Majlis to approve a new loan
from Russia.

Unfortunately, Atabak was murdered on August 31, 1907, the
same day that the British and Russians signed the Anglo-Russian Convention, an agreement specifying which countries would dominate
which parts of Persia. The Russian zone had most of the natural resources and major cities, while the British zone and neutral zone
served primarily as buffer states to keep the Russians away from India.

The people were outraged by the Anglo-Russian Convention, and
the Persian government never accepted it. Many people blamed Shah
Muhammad Ali, and an assassination attempt was made in 1908. He
survived and became more cooperative in working with the Majlis.
Persia was still insolvent, but it was beginning to function as a constitutional monarchy. Both the king and the legislature had power, each

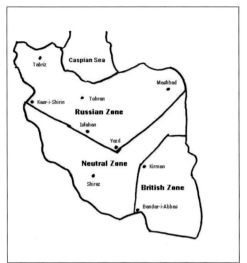

The Anglo-Russian Accord of 1907 divided Persia into zones of influence. The Russians got the wealthy cities and most natural resources, while the British got two buffer zones between the Russians and India.

side having to compromise to get some of what it wanted in return. On the pathway of political evolution, Persia pulled past Russia, which was then ruled by an absolute monarch with no independent legislature. This change upset the Russians tremendously, and in June of 1908, the Russians invaded Persia, attacked the Majlis, and put it out of business. Rebellions broke out all over, and the fighting continued for more than a year.

On July 13, 1909, Persian nationalist forces snuck into Tehran and conquered the city by surprise. They forced the Russian occupation troops to remain in their barracks, but did not mistreat them. After three days of intense negotiations with the Russians, Shah Muhammad Ali was formally deposed and his twelve-year-old son, Sultan Ahmad Mirza, became Ahmad Shah, the last ruler of the Qajari dynasty. The real power was wielded by the regent, Azudu'l- Mulk.

Britain and Russia formally recognized the new government, and on November 15, 1909, the Majlis reopened. The constitutional monarchy was once again open for business. The Russians still hated it, feared it, and were determined to destroy it. It took them two years.

The Russians attacked the Majlis again in November 1911. The constitutional government formally ended on December 24, 1911, and all political power returned to the shah. Democracy disappeared from Persia and still has not been restored more than ninety years later. Ironically, the Russians used an American as one of their excuses for invading.

Colonel Reza Khan

The American, Morgan Shuster, had been hired by the Majlis to rebuild the Persian treasury, which was bankrupt. They wanted someone who was not aligned with any of the European nations then exploiting them. They hired him to be the treasurer-general of Persia for a three-year term beginning in November 1910[6].

The Russians tried to get the United States State Department to block the appointment. The State Department asked the British how they regarded it. The British were annoyed with Russia for signing the Potsdam Agreement with the Germans so they said they had no objection.

Shuster and his American staff arrived in Tehran and got to work. They avoided meddling in politics, they solved a food shortage, and they got the Majlis to abolish an unpopular salt tax. They soon became very popular with the Persian people.

The Russians wanted to get rid of Shuster without killing him, which would have provoked a strong response from President Taft. Instead, they began making unreasonable demands, which escalated to an ultimatum that demanded the immediate firing of Shuster and a promise by the Persian government never to hire foreign citizens without first getting permission from Russia and Great Britain.

The Majlis voted unanimously to reject the Russian demands and stand up for national sovereignty and self-determination. The Persian people felt strongly the same way, and the courage of the Majlis members was widely praised.

Unfortunately, Russia had much greater military strength than Persia. Thousands of Russian troops poured into the country, and the Majlis was dissolved once again. Shuster resigned and returned to America. He was the first treasurer in decades to build a positive cash balance in the treasury. After he left there was fierce competition to see who could steal it. One of the banks won, and the country was officially insolvent once again.

This tragic event is an important moment in Iranian history. The Iranian people expressed a strong desire for a democratic form of government and, like the American revolutionaries of 1776, risked their lives, fortunes, and sacred honor for it. They looked to America for help, but the United States was not in a position to help the Iranian people in 1911. The situation is different now. Today the Iranian people are under siege from their own ruling class, the Khomeini outlaw regime, and the United States is capable of helping them fight for the democracy they want. The Khomeini outlaw regime is a threat to the United States and every other nation in Europe and the Americas, and most of the nations of Asia and Africa as well.

When World War I began, the Persians were sympathetic to the German cause, but avoided taking sides, even after the Germans asked them to enter into an alliance.

German agents in Persia stirred up trouble for the British and Russians, and the resulting fighting caused enough damage that crop yields declined. The foreign soldiers were able to pay more money than the poorer Persians could for the relatively scarce food supplies, and many Persians starved to death.

By avoiding an alliance with the Germans or Turks, Ahmad Shah kept his throne after the war ended. He remained the ruler of Persia until 1925, although he spent many of those years in Paris. After the war the czar of Russia was overthrown and his Soviet successors tried to conquer portions of Iran near the Russian border. They were successfully resisted by the Persian army under the leadership of Colonel Reza Khan.

Colonel Khan began reorganizing the army so that centralized power could be established. Many of the provinces were independent of the government in Tehran then. Ahmad Shah spent much of his time in Europe, partying and avoiding the difficult issues and problems back home.

The British became increasingly unhappy with Ahmad Shah and decided they wanted Colonel Khan to run the country. The first stage of a coup took place in February 1921. Colonel Khan became the minister of war and successfully negotiated a withdrawal of the Russian troops from the country later that same year.

He gradually worked his way up the Persian governmental hierarchy over the next few years. He was ultimately crowned the new Shah of Iran in April 1926, with the enthusiastic support of the Majlis and, more importantly, the British government.

Ahmad Shah resented the loss of his throne but was never willing to fight to get it back. He preferred life at the Hotel Majestic in Paris. His mother, Queen Malekeh Jahan, was a little more persistent. She left Europe for Persia, to see what she could do to restore the Qajari dynasty.

After many months and numerous adventures, she met in Baghdad with a representative of Prime Minister Khan (before his coronation as shah), who offered her three million tumans and a rent-free palace in Tehran. She did not trust him, so she turned down the offer and settled in Beirut. Ahmed Shah stayed in Paris and never returned to Persia. Thus ended the Qajari dynasty.

Once firmly in power, Colonel Khan took the new name Reza Shah Pahlavi and pursued an aggressive program of modernization. He felt that rapid westernization was essential, in order to promote national unity, reduce poverty, and lessen foreign interference. Under his rule a white collar middle class and a blue collar working class emerged for the first time[7].

He had both successes and failures. He succeeded in restoring national unity and centralized control, but was unable to get out of the Soviet-Iranian Treaty of Friendship of 1921, which gave the Soviet Union the right to invade Iran if a third party invaded or tried to use Iran as a base for attacking Russia.

He built hospitals, the University of Tehran, and the Trans-Iranian Railway. He made primary school education mandatory and sent Iranian college students to Europe for further education. He established a secular justice system with real judges, and about ninety percent of the Islamic clerics lost their judicial functions.

These steps pleased most Persians, but he also did things that annoyed them. In 1935 he changed the name of the country to Iran, and in 1936 he outlawed the chadoor. This angered not only the clerics

Col. Khan after he became the Shah. His greatness is often underestimated, because he was never able to break the country free of the British and Russians.

but also many women, who felt that the government was forcing them to dress like prostitutes. His son, Shah Reza II, later revoked the ban so that women could wear whatever they wanted.

Shah Reza I eventually got into major conflicts with the British over oil. Prior to the twentieth century oil had relatively little commercial value, but it became a major export. Iran is located in a region that contains seventy percent of the world's known oil and almost sixty percent of its natural gas, so it is not surprising that once oil became a valuable commodity, conflict would arise.

In 1901, a British explorer obtained a sixty-year monopoly on exploring, drilling, transporting, and selling oil. The monopoly was taken over by the Anglo-Persian Oil Company (later renamed the Anglo-Iranian Oil Company, then British Petroleum, and now BP). Oil was discovered in Khuzistan in 1908, and production was under way by 1912.

Oil was a profitable business, but most of the profits went to the Anglo-Persian Oil Company. This was upsetting to the Iranian people, who felt that they should be making most of the profit, not the British.

In 1932 Reza I canceled the British oil rights, but the British forced him to reinstate them and extend them for another sixty years. The British still ruled India and could have invaded Iran from there, so his decision to back down was sensible.

After World War II began, the British asked the shah to deport all the Germans in the country, on the grounds that they were sent to sabotage British oil production. He refused, on the grounds that he needed them for his development projects. That was a mistake.

In August of 1941, Britain and the Soviet Union invaded Iran, arrested Reza I, and sent him into exile in South Africa. This enabled them to seize control of the Trans-Iranian Railroad and transport supplies to the Soviets. In 1942 the Soviets took eleven tons of Iranian gold and $11,000,000 in Iranian currency back to Moscow for safekeeping and, predictably, failed to return any of it after the war.

After the gold, oil, and military control were secure, Mohammad Reza Pahlavi, the son of Reza Shah, was allowed to become the new shah. The British and Soviet forces kept the Iranian oil fields out of German hands, and the country was so securely controlled that during the war Churchill, Roosevelt, and Stalin held a summit conference in Tehran.

Reza Shah died in exile in 1944. World War II ended in 1945, when the Japanese surrendered to the Americans. The British troops left Iran soon after, but the Soviets stayed until May 1946. The new shah kept a low profile on the oil issue and managed to avoid upsetting the British. Some other Iranian politicians were not so agreeable, however, and it became a hot button issue for several years.

This painting shows Churchill leading Roosevelt and Stalin in a charge against Hitler, Hirohito, and Mussolini. It was given to Churchill during the Tehran summit conference. Roosevelt and Stalin received similar paintings showing each of them leading the charge. Mussolini is shown thrown from his horse; the Italian army had disbanded about 60 days before the conference, when the Allied forces landed at Salerno.

Chapter 3

Iran from World War II to 1979

The oil monopoly of the Anglo-Iranian Oil Company continued after World War II, but in the late '40s it came under attack from an Iranian politician named Muhammad Mossadegh. He demanded the nationalization of all Iranian oil fields. He became so popular that the shah was eventually forced to appoint him prime minister.

After becoming prime minister, Mossadegh approached the British for an increased Iranian share of the oil field profits. The British played hardball, and instead of negotiating, they withdrew from the oil refineries. They thought that the Iranians couldn't run them on their own. But they could and did.

Mossadegh had support from the Tudeh (Iran's communist party), Iranian nationalists, and wealthy Iranian landowners who opposed the shah's early attempts at land reform. The Tudeh was strongly allied with the Soviet Union, which stood to benefit if the British lost their oil monopoly.

The British put pressure on Western countries to boycott Iranian oil, and they honored the boycott. Mossadegh then tried to sell the oil to the Soviet Union in 1952.

At that time the Soviets were improving their hydrogen bomb, making waves in Germany, supporting the North Koreans in the Korean War, and causing people to wonder whether they were going to

Shah Mohammad Reza Pahlavi and Empress Farah Diba

invade Western Europe. The prospect of the Soviets gaining control of Iran's oil greatly intensified these concerns.

In the colonial era, the British would have sent the army into Iran to talk sense to Mossadegh, but they couldn't do that in 1952. They no longer had military bases in India or Pakistan, which had both gained independence. They made plans to invade Iran with 70,000 troops, but the plans were never carried out. Instead, the British turned to the Americans for help, implying that Mossadegh was about to turn Iran into a communist nation.

President Eisenhower did not see Mossadegh as a communist leader, but he thought that there was a serious danger Mossadegh would hand over control of the country to the Soviet Union, becoming nothing more than a Soviet puppet. This would have been a strategic disaster, giving the Soviets control over the Iranian oil fields, the Persian Gulf, and the Shatt-al-Arab waterway, which oil tankers must pass through on their way to Europe, the United States, or Japan. This acquisition would also have given Stalin, the Soviet dictator, enough fuel for an enormous fleet of tanks to invade Western Europe. There were no German army forces in 1952, and the combined French, British, and American forces would have been far too small to defeat a massive Soviet tank invasion if it came.

This risk was intolerable, so President Eisenhower instructed the CIA to prepare contingency plans to overthrow Mossadegh. In August of 1953, Mossadegh tried to make himself a virtual dictator. He dissolved the Majlis and ignored all orders from the shah. The CIA contacted key Iranian generals, and by August 19, Mossadegh was out of a job. He was tried and sentenced to death, but the shah commuted the sentence to a prison term.

He then took steps to strengthen his control and prevent another Mossadegh from ever arising. He built a strong army, navy, and air force, and made sure that he had constant favorable press coverage. Loyal supporters were generously rewarded, while opponents were jailed. Over time these measures succeeded in strengthening the military and the shah's control. His government became strong and stable but also allowed corruption to grow.

In 1963 the Shah began the White Revolution, which included agrarian reform from the top down. The "White" meant that he would revolutionize the country without spilling a drop of blood. In order to rally popular support, a national referendum was held, and on January 26, 1963, the Iranian people voted in favor of the White Revolution.

It had six main components:

1. People who owned more than one village could keep one but had to sell the rest of their villages to the government. The government would then give out parcels to local peasants.

2. The government would sell a number of state-run enterprises to private investors.

3. Forests and some pasture land were nationalized.

4. Workers and employees would become shareholders in the companies they worked for.

5. Women could vote and run for office.

6. A Literacy Corps, composed of high school graduates, was sent out to the villages to increase the literacy rate.

Within two years, 8,200 villages had been taken and divided up among 300,000 peasant families. The clergy were strongly opposed to this reform, because it cut into their wealth indirectly. Iranian landowners used to make generous contributions to religious institutions. Many mullahs received large properties and lived very well. These gifts dried up when the landowners had to sell off their excess villages, which infuriated the mullahs. Some of the peasant families were unable to succeed at farming their own land because they had no training

Prime Minister Mossadegh

in agricultural economics. This fact was later used to criticize the plan and claim it had failed.

The mullahs also opposed other parts of the White Revolution. Hojatolislam Khomeini (who later became Ayatollah Khomeini) wrote to the shah complaining about giving women the right to vote. The clergy thought this was a terrible idea, and when the shah refused to give ground, they began organizing protests and riots. By the time things quieted down, about fifty people had died.

The shah's reforms, combined with ambitious public works programs and industrial expansion, brought an economic boom to Iran. According to the shah's former budget director, Dr. Abdolmadjid Madjidi, Iran's rate of growth between 1963 and 1973 was 11.2 percent, while inflation was only 1.25 percent[8].

During this same period Iran was in the midst of a population explosion. It grew from twenty-three million people in 1963 to thirty-five million in 1977, an increase of fifty percent in fourteen years. There was a tremendous migration of people from the countryside into the cities, much like England at the beginning of its industrial growth.

The shah loved European and American culture, and he continued to introduce elements of it into Iranian society. Some of these attempts further antagonized the Islamic clergy, such as separating church and state, legalizing abortion, instituting daylight-savings time, and abolishing the Islamic calendar.

He also issued a decree granting diplomatic immunity to all American soldiers stationed in Iran, and Khomeini became famous for his criticisms of this order. The shah deported Khomeini in 1964, but he became even more influential during his years in exile.

The shah held power for thirty-eight years, a long time by histori-cal standards, but over time people began to forget his successes and remember the things that irritated them. This trend grew throughout the 1970s, while the shah became progressively weaker due to cancer of the blood.

The shah also had enemies outside Iran. He antagonized the Amer-icans and Europeans by causing OPEC to double the price of oil in the early 1970s, resulting in inflation and economic disruption. He antag-onized the Arabs and many other Moslems by supplying Israel with oil during the Yom Kippur War of 1973.

The French government was among these enemies. Shortly after Khomeini moved to France, he wanted his house to be equipped with advanced communications. Within a few hours, he had two telex lines and six telephone lines, with which he could directly contact his agents in Tehran. A local recording studio was persuaded to abandon all its existing customers and do nothing but produce thousands of copies of Khomeini's taped speeches, messages, and interviews.

During his four months in France, Khomeini was able to give 132 interviews, issue fifty declarations, and speak to over 100,000 visi-tors[9].

The shah's most vocal enemies were the Islamic clergy: the mul-lahs, hojatolislams, and ayatollahs. In the mid 70s they built hundreds of mosques in Tehran and elsewhere, set up an independent banking system, and began training hundreds of thousands of students. This took a lot of money, some of which came from Iranians and much from outside the country, in particular the Persian Gulf states and some wealthy Saudi Arabian Moslems. It didn't occur to them that Khomeini could be a danger to their own governments until after he was in power and it was too late.

The internal Iranian opposition to Shah Reza II was largely unor-ganized until 1976 or 1977. However, the mullahs had been running an outreach program with other anti-shah groups, and by 1977 they had formed many alliances. Many Iranians were sick and tired of the shah's changes and wanted to restore the status quo. For many people, too much had changed too quickly.

The student demonstrations in November of 1977 were violent, but things became worse in the beginning of 1978. In January, the shah's government forced a newspaper to print a strongly anti-Khomeini article on the front page. The clerics responded with massive demonstrations and rioting in the city of Qom.

Demonstrations and riots began occurring in other cities, and by May of 1978, the government had to use tanks to put down rioting in Tehran. Violence and unrest continued to rise, and on August 19, Khomeini supporters locked more than 600 people in the Rex Cinema, a movie theater, and set fire to it. They were all burned alive.

Khomeini propagandists blamed the fire on the shah's government, and the mood of the Iranian people was already so anti-shah that the majority of them believed the lie. Even the middle class, which owed its existence to the shah and his father, would not support him.

The government's response to these crises was cautious, to minimize armed clashes. The shah had a sincere desire to avoid killing Iranian civilians, but the mullahs took that as a sign of weakness.

After the arson in the Rex Cinema, the shah adopted a more conciliatory tone. He fired his prime minister, moved his other cabinet ministers around, and hired four new ministers. Most of them were more traditional than his prior ministers, and they took steps to calm people down, such as restoring the Islamic calendar, shutting down casinos, and banning pornography. But they also allowed greater freedom of the press. Their enemies took advantage of this to increase their organizing and to coordinate riots and demonstrations. Khomeini's picture began to appear in newspapers again.

The calls for the shah's removal intensified, and the strikes and rioting continued. The shah declared martial law in September of 1978 and cracked down on demonstrators in Tehran and elsewhere. Two months later he again fired his prime minister and replaced him with a general, who headed up a new cabinet composed of other generals.

On September 8, heavy fighting took place in Tehran between soldiers and rioters, and quite a few people were killed. Further riots were expected the following week, but Khomeini urged his followers to stay off the streets and avoid clashing with the soldiers. The senior army officers were mostly loyal to the shah, but Khomeini hoped to

These tribal dancers were photographed before 1979, when dancing was still legal in Iran. Today Iranians almost never dance in public, for fear of being arrested and punished.

form alliances with some of them and gain followers among younger soldiers. The soldiers for their part did not enjoy shooting at Iranian citizens, and most of the time they avoided using excessive force.

In October of 1978 the shah proposed forming a new government with a member of the opposition as prime minister. Khomeini refused to negotiate with the shah and said that he would have nothing to do with anyone who did. The other opposition groups went along with Khomeini on the theory that his influence was so strong that no new government could survive without his support.

Things were going so badly that by December oil production in Iran had fallen from six million barrels a day to only 250,000. The same month, opposition forces gained control of a few towns and began setting up kangaroo courts and ordering the executions of army officers and members of the secret police.

The shah determined that the military solution was not working and went back to conciliation. On December 28, 1978, he appointed Shahpour Bakhtiar, a prominent opposition leader, as the new prime minister. Bakhtiar was an educated man who had served in the Iranian government under Mossadegh more than twenty years earlier. He had been arrested a number of times in the 1960s for his opposition to the shah's programs. He was wary of the religious extremists and believed that a coalition government was the best solution for the crisis. He wanted to take political power away from the shah while preserving

The Rex Cinema after the Khomeini arson.

the titular institution of monarchy, much like the modern kings and queens of England. He was willing to risk angering Khomeini, and he had impeccable credentials as an opposition leader. He was an excellent choice if the shah was hoping to create division and conflict among the various opposition groups. Unfortunately, Bakhtiar's colleagues sided with Khomeini and kicked Bakhtiar out of the party, describing his appointment as a superficial change.

Bakhtiar was a seasoned politician who knew he was taking a risk by accepting the job, and he imposed conditions before accepting it. He insisted that the shah leave the country for at least eighteen months, instruct the military to support Bakhtiar's government, and on his return agree to serve as a reigning monarch but without any governing power.

Once the deal was agreed upon, events moved swiftly. Bakhtiar announced his acceptance of the prime minister position on December 28, and on January 6, 1979, Bakhtiar announced his new cabinet. On January 16, 1979, the shah left Iran, saying that he was tired and needed a long vacation. He urged everyone to support the Bakhtiar government.

The shah's departure was celebrated all over Iran as an indication that he had gone into permanent exile. People pulled down statues of him, rejoicing that he was gone and looking forward to the restoration of freedom and civil liberties that Khomeini and his followers had long promised them. Few of them realized how much grief, torture, death, and misery would enter their lives.

One commentator has listed four main reasons why Iranians from all walks of life united to overthrow the Shah:

1. Unhappiness over fraud, corruption, and moral decay

2. Unpopular reform measures

3. Lack of independence from foreign countries

4. Social and economic injustices between the ruling class and the lower classes[10].

Three of these four factors are present in Iran today. Khomeini and his followers did establish Iran's independence from foreign countries, but the other three sources of popular discontent are all present and growing.

1. Fraud, corruption, and moral decay are still a problem. Statoil, a Norwegian oil company, entered into a contract to pay fifteen million dollars to Rafsanjani's son for consulting services in order to receive favorable oil treatment from Iran. The political system is so corrupt that non-Khomeini outlaw candidates are not even allowed to run. The government then proclaims a smashing victory for the Khomeini outlaw regime after the election, and some Western news media fall for the hoax.

2. Unpopular changes of the Khomeini outlaw regime are hated because they are barbaric and often stupid. The torture and rape of female prisoners before they are executed is not popular with the Iranian public. The new law that allows police and private militia members to shoot at passing cars is also unpopular. The laws banning satellites TV dishes, CDs, stereos, cosmetics, dancing, and playing cards are also unpopular. Right now the Majlis is working on a law to ban Western clothing. This law will be very unpopular if it is ever enacted.

3. Social injustice is also a prime source of public irritation. Veterans of the Iran-Iraq war receive inadequate pensions, millions of Iranians are homeless, unemployment is sky high, and there is unfair discrimination against women and Bahais. The recent execution of a rape victim, while the man who raped her only received 100 lashes, was widely seen as unjust.

Defense Minister and Rear Admiral Ali Shamkhani, a former candidate for the presidency of Iran.

The majority of Iranians today are under thirty and have been raised with Islamic values. They must be allowed to speak and to show what they can do.

But the Khomeini outlaw regime is afraid of them, afraid to trust them. Just as the shah was afraid to have generals that were too independent, so the Khomeini outlaw regime is afraid of Iranian youth who think for themselves. The Iranian people want Iran to be a free, independent, and prosperous country, one that all its neighbors envy. But the people running the government cannot believe in that, cannot trust in that, or perhaps cannot see a role for themselves in that.

Student demonstrations in Iran are often met with excessive violence by government and private forces. On July 9, 1999, pro-cleric private groups staged extraordinarily violent attacks on students in the dormitories at Tehran University. One student was killed, another twenty were injured, and entire walls of buildings were destroyed. Khatami aligned himself with Khamenei and the forces of evil, calling for an end to the demonstrations and claiming that the leaders were people with evil aims.

This led to nationwide protests, the worst in two decades. In subsequent years, marches and other commemorations of this event have occurred, with some of them marred by violence as well. The early protests focused on Khamenei, Rafsanjani, and the other so-called "hardline" clerics, but the 2003 student demonstrations criticized Khatami as well, for failing to live up to his promises.

Prime Minister Shahpour Bakhtiar

The attitude of the Iranian government was made clear by Defense Minister Ali Shamkhani in a statement on July 13, 1999:

"We will restore peace at any cost in Iran from Wednesday. All of the authorities agree that nobody should cross the three red lines of Islamic Rule, Velayat-e-Faqih [the non-Koranic doctrine of a pope-like infallible Supreme Leader], and Ayatollah Khamenei as the symbol of the first two pillars."

College students are not the only ones demonstrating against the regime. When the Iranian national soccer team does well in the World Cup elimination rounds, people from all walks of life come out into the streets of major cities to celebrate. They often shout anti-regime slogans or pro-American ones. In 2001 a crowd gathered in Tehran due to a false rumor that the government had ordered the Iranian team to deliberately lose a key game. The protestors shouted such heretical things as 'We love you, America!' and 'We love you, Reza Pahlavi!'"

If the Khomeini outlaw regime cannot trust its own children to lead Iran in a new direction, away from poverty, prostitution, disease, terrorism, and starvation, then the day will come when it will follow the Safavid and Afsharid dynasties into the dustbin of history.

Chapter 4

The 1979 Revolution

The first phase of the Iranian Revolution ended on January 16, 1979, when the shah left Iran, never to return. This was probably the happiest phase for most of the revolutionaries, because everyone was still working together toward a common goal.

Khomeini returned to Iran in February of 1979, and before the end of the year he had defeated, converted, killed, or driven off all his rivals. The people with the greatest chance of defeating him, the shah's generals, were surprisingly easy to conquer. Most of them surrendered without a fight.

It may seem odd that the shah's generals did not fight to protect the Bakhtiar government from Khomeini's forces, or stage a massive military coup, the way Nader Shah or Shah Reza I would have done. Hundreds of thousands, perhaps even millions of lives might have been saved, and the Iraq-Iran War might have been prevented or greatly shortened. But this did not happen. Khomeini encouraged the generals to think that if they cooperated, they would have places in the new government. Once he gained power, they were slaughtered ruthlessly.

Regrettably, the United States is partly to blame for this. In January 1979, President Carter sent an American general to Iran to convince the shah to leave the country and to convince the generals not to stage a coup. He did nothing to help Bakhtiar hold on to the country. Khomeini refused to negotiate with Bakhtiar, and his charisma was so

Khomeini executed all the men in this picture. Empress Farah Diba is still alive.

powerful that he persuaded Bakhtiar's own political party to turn against him.

On February 5, 1979, Khomeini appointed Mehdi Bazargan as the new prime minister of Iran, while Bakhtiar was still in office! This led to armed clashes between Khomeini followers and the army, which at that time was still following the shah's orders to support the Bakhtiar government. That state of affairs lasted less than a week.

On February 11, 1979, the army withdrew its support of Bakhtiar and declared it would remain neutral in the fighting. Bakhtiar promptly resigned and fled to Paris. He continued to fight the Khomeini outlaw regime and give hope to Iranians overseas for twelve years, until he was brutally killed by Iranian government assassins in 1991.

After defeating Bakhtiar, Khomeini spent the rest of 1979 consolidating his power. A referendum was held in March on whether to establish an Islamic government, without specifying what form of Islamic government (e.g., dictatorship, oligarchy, democracy). The referendum passed by a large majority, and in December a new constitution was approved. Elections were held for the presidency and Majlis, and in September 1980 a formal cabinet was formed. None of this reduced Khomeini's power, but it helped to keep up appearances.

On November 4, 1979, Khomeini endorsed the kidnapping of the US Embassy hostages in Tehran. Bazargan resigned the next day.

Khomeini praised him for his faithful service and sincere religious beliefs. This probably saved his life. The Iranian government murdered several other former prime ministers but left Bazargan alone. He died peacefully in old age.

Throughout 1979 and 1980, the alliances between Khomeini's supporters and the other anti-shah groups weakened and deteriorated. Slowly the other groups lost influence, and by 1984 all serious contenders for political power had to join Khomeini's party and choose between the two main factions, headed by Khamenei and Rafsanjani. Both men reported to Khomeini as the supreme Islamic authority, and in public they expressed strong mutual support and admiration. They have known each other since 1957, and they can handle competition and disagreements without letting it damage their relationship.

By 1984 Khamenei had become the president and Rafsanjani had become the speaker of the Majlis.

In the 1984 elections only candidates loyal to Khomeini were allowed to run. Everyone else was taken off the ballot by the Council of Guardians, a group of senior Islamic clerics. In one election, more than 2300 candidates were disqualified. The same screening procedure is used today.

In 1988 Rafsanjani was elected president, as Khamenei was termed out under the Iranian constitution. Rafsanjani served two full terms as president, ending in 1997, at which time Khatami ran for president and defeated the favored candidate, Ali Akbar Nateq-Nouri. His margin of victory was so huge that it overwhelmed the usual ballot-stuffing. Khatami was reelected in 2001 and will be termed out in 2005.

Rafsanjani has hinted that he might run for president again. How he will get around the term limits problem is unclear. Perhaps Khamenei will issue a fatwa, or perhaps the Council of Guardians will disqualify all the other candidates. Perhaps he will try to get a constitutional amendment passed.

In a fair election Rafsanjani would lose. Not that many Iranians like him, if they ever did. He barely won reelection to the Majlis the last time he ran. But in the Khomeini outlaw regime, he is still one of the top two rulers, and his power will continue unabated regardless of form in which it is manifested.

Chapter 5

Khomeini, Torture, and Terror

For thousands of years, governments in Central Asia have used torture, killing, and imprisonment to get their way. Iran was no exception, and the extent and severity of the brutality varied from one government to the next.

Shah Reza II was toward the mild end of the range by historical standards. The conditions in his prisons were far superior to Khomeini's prisons, according to Ayatollah Montazeri, a loyal Khomeini supporter for many years. This fact is sometimes overlooked by critics of the shah. He had more press coverage than prior rulers, which made even the slightest blemishes visible.

Khomeini and his followers were at the other end of the spectrum. They enjoyed torture and killing, and they did it for their own amusement as well as for power.

The killing started almost immediately after Khomeini gained power. One of his first targets was the shah's generals and other senior military officers. The killings of these men continued up to the beginning of the Iraq-Iran War in 1980. At that point many of the lower-ranking air force pilots were still alive, so they were released from prison to take part in the aerial warfare with Iraq. They did a great job, and together with the army, they drove Saddam's troops back into Iraq.

Saddam tried to negotiate a peace treaty, but Khomeini refused to negotiate. He wanted to conquer Iraq, add Iraqi Shi'ite troops to his

Khomeini

army, and keep going until he controlled Israel, Jordan, Saudi Arabia, and every country in the area that was not already an ally. The cost in human life did not deter him but rather excited him, particularly the deaths of people and ethnic groups he did not like.

This victory was denied Khomeini. In 1988 he finally gave up on the Iraq-Iran War and entered into a peace treaty with Iraq. He died in 1989, on the bad-luck day of the 13th of Khordad, without ever realizing his dream of conquering the Middle East and beginning an Islamic crusade against Europe and the Americas.

Khomeini's dreams of conquest were presented to the public in a slightly different way, that of conquering the world for Islam, not for Khomeini, in order to disguise his personal greed and ambition. The trick worked. Almost everyone in the West viewed Khomeini as a sincere religious fanatic rather than a greedy politician with a fondness for murder, torture, and genocide. Some of the less educated, rural Iranians also fell for it. Most educated and urban Iranians, though, saw through the disguise within a year after he came to power.

Khomeini's extreme ambition was noticed as early as 1963, when he was placed under house arrest for trying to overthrow the shah's government. At that time General Hassan Pakravan, the head of the SAVAK intelligence agency, had lunch with him once a week. About fifteen years later, the General described Khomeini in a memorable conversation with his wife. As she recounts it,

"I asked my husband, 'What was the object of your conversation [with the ayatollah]? What did you talk about?' He said, 'Well, about religion, about philosophy, about history.' I said, 'Is he a very learned

General Pakravan, who saved Khomeini's life and was later executed on Khomeini's orders.

man?' He said, 'Well, his religion I cannot say, because I'm not a religious person. I suppose he is, because he is a specialist. But his ignorance in history and philosophy is something unbelievable. You know, the man who said America oppressed Iran for the last twenty-five centuries.' My husband said, 'He's very, very, very ignorant.' I said, 'But what struck you in him? What did you find was the most striking aspect of his temperament or his character?' He said, 'His ambition.' I said, 'Ambition? What do you mean ambition? What kind of ambition, political, religious?' He said, 'I couldn't find out, because he's very secretive.' Then he said, 'You know, it made my hair stand on end. It was frightening.' " [11]

General Pakravan is one of the few pro-Western non-clerics who got to know Khomeini this well. Khomeini charmed him, so well that when Khomeini was sentenced to death by an Iranian court, General Pakravan interceded with the shah to save his life. The shah hated the idea but finally gave in after much arguing. He told the general to find a way to do it without setting aside the court's ruling.

The general consulted Ayatollah Shariatmadari, who came up with a solution: make Khomeini an ayatollah. So instead of executing Khomeini, they promoted him to the most powerful and prestigious level of Islamic cleric. Khomeini showed his gratitude by stirring up more trouble and was exiled to Turkey in 1964. From there he wrote a polite letter to the shah, asking permission to move to Najaf, Iraq, to study religion further.

The Khomeini charm worked again, and the request was granted. Khomeini stayed in Iraq until the mid-70s, when revolutionary activity began to heat up in Iran. At that time the shah persuaded Saddam

This man killed Ali Akbar Tabatabai for $4,000 and a one-way ticket to Switzerland. He is seen here in his movie role.

Hussein to kick him out, and Khomeini moved to France. His power and influence increased tremendously there, and when he returned to Iran in 1979 he was given a hero's welcome. All of this was possible only because General Pakravan saved his life in 1963.

After Khomeini came to power, he had General Pakravan executed[12].

Khomeini also tried to kill any civilians who might pose a threat to him and his government. His first intended targets outside Iran were big ones: the shah's family, former Prime Minister Bakhtiar, and Ali Akbar Tabatabai, Khomeini's most prominent critic in the United States.

The shah's wife and children were too well-guarded to reach, but Princess Ashraf, the shah's sister, was not. They sent a single assassin, who failed to get her but did get her son, Prince Shahriar Shafiq. The killer saw him on a street in Paris, came up from behind, shot him twice in the head, and fled[13].

In July 1980, Khomeini's killers tried to assassinate former Prime Minister Bakhtiar, who was also in Paris. In a pattern used to this day, the Iranian government planned and financed the attack, but hired foreign terrorists to carry it out. They killed one of Bakhtiar's guards and one of his neighbors, but Bakhtiar himself was unhurt. The lead killer went to jail and remained there until July 27, 1990, when French President Mitterand ordered him released[14].

The Iranian government did not make another publicly known attempt against Bakhtiar for more than ten years. On August 6, 1991, they tried again, and this time they succeeded. They sent a three-man hit squad, let by Mohammad Azadi, a senior officer in the Special Operations Committee, the branch of the Iranian government that plans and organizes assassinations. The actual timing of a killing is usually decided by Khamenei and Rafsanjani, but once the order to kill is given, Special Operations carries it out promptly and efficiently.

Three killers entered Bakhtiar's home as guests; Bakhtiar knew one of them personally. They murdered him and his secretary in a particularly gruesome way. Afterward, they escaped from France with the help of other conspirators.

The French prosecuted the crime, but only two people served serious jail time: Massoud Hendi, who prepared the travel documents, and Ali Vakili Rad, one of the hit men. Mohammad Azadi made it back to Iran, and the third hit man disappeared.

Bakhtiar and his secretary were not the only people murdered by the Iranian government on French soil. Other victims include:

General Gholam-Ali Oveissi and his brother, Gholam-Hossein (murdered in 1984)

Cyrus Elahi, a pro-democracy activist and member of the Flag of Freedom Organization (murdered in 1990)

Abdol-Rahman Boroumand, an adviser to Bakhtiar (murdered in 1991)

Reza Mazlouman, a writer and political activist (murdered in 1996)[15]

The Iranian government never suffered any serious consequences from these murders. No matter what they did, the French kept on doing business with them. And business has been good. By 2003 France was selling two billion euros a year of goods and services to Iran.[16]

Germany has also responded ineffectively to Iranian terrorism. The Iranian government has murdered at least six people in Germany in the last twenty-five years, and they have suffered no serious consequences.

The most famous of the German murder victims was Fereydoun Farokhzad, an internationally known singer. In August of 1992, the Iranian government's killers stabbed him to death at his home in Bonn and left him lying in his own blood. The killers were never brought to justice.

Singer Fereydoun Farokhzad, murdered by the Khomeini outlaw regime due to his outspoken political views.

The following month Iranian terrorists shot and killed Sadegh Sharafkandi, Fatah Abdoli, Homayoun Ardalan, and Nouri Dehkordi at the Mykonos Restaurant in Berlin. The killers were eight Lebanese and one Iranian, Kazem Darabi. The Germans caught him and four of the Lebanese and put them on trial.

The German investigators discovered that Ali Fallahian, the Minster of Intelligence for Iran at the time, was involved. They issued an arrest warrant for him, which the Iranian government refused to honor, despite a finding by trial court judge Frithjof Kubsch that the murders were ordered at the highest state levels.

The four victims were part of a Kurdish separatist movement previously led by Abdol-Rahman Ghassemlou, who was killed by Iranian government terrorists in Austria in 1989. The Austrian police arrested the killers, but saw their work undone when the Austrian government later released all three of them and allowed them to return to Iran[17].

It was during the Mykonos Restaurant trial that people outside Iran first learned that the Special Operations Committee plans these murders and then puts them on the shelf until Khamenei or Rafsanjani orders the killing carried out.

The Iranian government has murdered people in other European countries as well.

Bijan Fazeli (Great Britain, 1986) was killed by a bomb in his video store in Kensington. His father had produced a number of comedy shows depicting mullahs as corrupt and evil. The following year another Iranian expatriate, Behrouz Bagheri, was killed by a fire bomb in his shop in Paris.

Mohammad-Ali Tavakoli-Nabavi and his son Noureddin were pro-shah demonstrators living in England. They were shot outside their home in Wembley[18].

Kamran Hedayati, an active member of the Kurdish Democratic Party, received a letter bomb at his home in Stockholm, Sweden. He survived but lost his senses of sight and smell[19].

Professor Kazem Radjavi was murdered in Switzerland in 1990. The Swiss judge issued thirteen arrest warrants but could not get co-operation from Iran. Two of the suspects were being held in France, but he could not get cooperation from France either. Due to insufficient evidence, the case never went to trial.

The Italians had a similar problem in 1993, when the Iranian government killed Mohammad-Hossein Naghdim, a member of the National Council of Resistance, in Rome. Five years later, the Italian authorities still did not have enough evidence to go to trial[20].

In Bucharest, Romania, Assadi Mohammad Ali was murdered by the Iranian government on November 12, 1994. Three men burst into his apartment, and one of them plunged a sword into his back. His widow recognized one of the killers as a member of the Iranian embassy staff.

The timidity of European governments in the face of Iranian terrorism has been appalling. It appears to have several causes: weak armed forces, low birth rates among non-Moslem citizens, fear of losing valuable imports of oil and natural gas, and intimidation on the part of the Iranian government itself.

The Islamic Republic exerted pressure on the Europeans in a number of ways. These included kidnapping their citizens on fake charges and releasing them in exchange for Iranian officials arrested in Europe. The Islamic authorities also organized raids on various European embassies, beating up staff, seizing documents and setting parts of buildings on fire. In one case, the French ambassador, Guy Georgy, was held hostage until France allowed an Iranian terror mastermind to leave Paris before he could be arrested.

The number of Iranian Government murder victims in Asia is even higher than in Europe, and some of the killings are on a larger scale. In Pakistan in 1987 Iranian government terrorists wounded twenty-three bystanders in the course of killing Faramarz-Aghai and Ali-Reza Pourshafizadeh. The following year another terrorist began shooting at Iranian refugees waiting in line at the headquarters of the United Nations High Commissioner for Refugees in Karachi, killing one and wounding five others.

The Iranian government has taken particular delight in terror strikes against the Saudi Arabian government. The Saudi victims include

Abdul Ghani Bedawi (Ankara, Turkey, 1985; Saudi Embassy employee),

Saleh Abdullah al-Maliki (Bangkok, Thailand, 1989; Saudi Embassy employee),

Abdurrahman Shrewi (Ankara, Turkey, 1989; Saudi military attache),

Ali al-Marzuq (West Beirut, Lebanon, 1989; last remaining Saudi diplomat in the country),

Abdalrahman al-Basri, Fahd Abdallah al-Bahli, and Ahmad Abdallah al-Sayf (Bangkok, Thailand, 1990; Saudi intelligence agents)[21]

The Iranian government also murders people inside Iran. A recent example is the murder on November 21, 2003, of Dariush Foruhar and his wife Parvaneh. The killers cut off his head and one of her breasts.

Another example is the killing of Ali Reza Merkand in Zanjan on August 15, 1994. He was shot by government security forces while leaving a hospital where his mother had just been admitted. No one knows why they did it.

Many killings in Iran are also carried out by private militias. In 1994, the Majlis enacted a law allowing both government policemen and the Bassiji (private militia) to shoot demonstrators. They can also shoot at cars if they think the occupants have stolen goods or drugs. They are exempt from any civil or criminal liability for these shootings. If innocent people are killed, their relatives can theoretically seek compensation from the Iranian government, but few Iranians would

Zahra Kazemi, an Iranian-Canadian photographer who was beaten to death by the Iranian government.

be foolish enough to call government attention to themselves for any reason.

Homicide is not the only means the Iranian government uses to keep its citizens under its thumb. Torture is also quite widely employed.

One of the prominent torturers of the Khomeini era was "the Butcher of Evin," Assadollah Lajevardi, who at one time ran the Evin Prison. He was murdered in the Tehran bazaar in August of 1998, on the tenth anniversary of the killing of more than 8,000 prisoners on the personal orders of Khomeini.

After Lajevardi's death, President Khatami described him as "a valiant son of Islam and revolution, a servant of the regime and the people." Most people would disagree. One of Lajevardi's prisoner-victims recalled him this way:

"He was the symbol of fear. His face radiated with sheer brutality. Once, when some prisoners complained that eighty of them were piled up in a room built for six, he coldly promised to see to it within hours by executing some and transferring others to another jail worse than Evin. And he did exactly what he had said. That night, some of us were executed," recalled one prisoner who spent four years with Mr. Lajevardi.[22]

According to an earlier Iranian president, Abdolhasan Bani-sadr, Lajevardi was eliminating 500 to 1000 political prisoners a day at the height of the executions.

Lajaverdi claimed to have created more than 170 new forms of torture. One of these, called "dog box," was a hole 2 feet 3 inches by 3 feet. The prisoner would be forced to sit there cross-legged. According to Amir Entezam, a deputy prime minister who spent more than sixteen years in Khomeini's prisons, a few days of sitting in that position would cause the prisoner to become totally paralyzed.

Saaed Mortazavi, the chief prosecutor for Tehran and the man most widely believed to have killed Zahra Zakemi

The most frightening of the tortures was called the coffin. They simply put the prisoner in a coffin, closed the door on top of him, and left him there. This form of torture usually resulted in incurable insanity.

Deputy Prime Minister Entezam paid a heavy price for disclosing these things to the public. He had previously spent 1979 through 1996 in prison, on a conviction for spying for the United States. His sentence was suspended in 1996, but after his criticisms of Lajevardi, it was reinstated and he went back to Evin Prison. A court order for his release was ignored or rescinded; it is not clear which, because the Iranian government refused to explain it to his wife, to let her see him, or to let him see a lawyer.[23]

Lajevardi was feared by all decent Iranians but very popular with the Khomeini outlaw regime. The Khomeini insiders who expressed regret and sorrow at Lajevardi's death included Khatami, Rafsanjani, Nateq Nouri and Mohammad Yazdi. Khomeini outlaw regime members may disagree with each other on some issues, but when it came to the death of the Butcher of Evin they were in complete agreement. They spoke with one voice in honoring the tradition of butchery, torture, and killing that Khomeini ordered and Lajevardi carried out.

Lajevardi was not the only butcher in Iran. The Iranian government has torturers of both sexes, many of whom have developed sick specialties of their own.

Hamid Baneshi ties his victims down horizontally, then beats on the top and bottom of their shoes simultaneously, until they pass out. The feet swell and become infected. Most of the victims are executed soon after that.

Zahra Kazemi's mother on the day Defendant Mohammad Ahmadi was acquitted of the murder of her daughter. Saeed Mortazavi has never been prosecuted for this crime.

Hassan Be Be specializes in burning people alive in ovens.

Zinat Saberi a female torturer, specializes in torture with cables.

Shahrokh Sabouri specializes in rape and burying people in mass graves while they are still alive.

Javad Moalem has the same specialties as Sabouri with an additional twist. He once placed a group of live prisoners into a grave, added explosives, covered them with dirt, then blew them up.

Fatemeh Jabari, a female torturer, helps decide when and how women are raped, tortured, and killed at Evin prison[24].

Lajevardi has been dead for more than five years, but nothing has changed since then. On June 23, 2003, an Iranian-Canadian photographer named Zahra Kazemi was arrested for taking photographs of demonstrators outside Evin Prison[25]. She was tortured and beaten so badly that her skull was broken. She died on July 10, 2003[26].

The Iranian government initially claimed she had died from a stroke, but a special commission appointed by Khatami later reported the cause of death as a "fractured skull, brain hemorrhage and its consequences resulting from a hard object hitting the head or the head

An artist's conception of how Atefeh might have looked if she had lived and if Iranian women were allowed to wear their hair as they please, without governmental regulations.

Atefeh on the day of her hanging. Witnesses say that she cried "Repentance" as they dragged her to the gallows. Under Islamic law, this cry is supposed to postpone the execution. Haji Reza ignored it and had her killed immediately.

hitting a hard object." Ms. Kazemi's relatives say that the torturers broke her fingers, nose, and toes and that there were burn marks on her chest[28]. The Canadian government withdrew its ambassador to Iran in protest, but that had little impact. Ms. Kazemi was a citizen of both countries, which limited what Canada could do under international law. Iran has a much stronger and newer navy than Canada, and its population is more then three times as large. It is doubtful that a Canadian trade embargo would strike terror in the hearts of the Iranian government, and it would have no impact on sales of Iranian oil[29].

It appears that Ms. Kazemi was not killed by the usual prison torture crew but rather by other Iranian government employees. Suspicion has been cast on Said Mortazavi, who specializes in harassing foreign journalists[30] and who fabricated the initial story of a stroke, according to Iranian government spokesman Mohammad Hussein Khoshvaqt[31].

Criminal proceedings were instituted against another Iranian government employee, a counterespionage agent named Mohammad

Reza Aghdam Ahmadi, but the trial was halted on July 17, 2004, after only three sessions[32]. One week later, on July 24, 2004, a verdict was issued finding Mr. Ahmadi innocent of all charges[33]. It is not clear whether Mr. Ahmadi had anything to do with Ms. Kazemi's treatment or was simply the target of a sham prosecution by some other government official who had a grudge against him.

Ms. Kazemi is by no means the only recent victim of torture in Iran. Here is a small sampling of atrocities from early 2004.

February 26, 2004: Mohsen Mofidi, a thirty-five-year old man, died a few days after receiving eighty lashes in prison for possessing a satellite dish and medicine containing alcohol[34]. The Iranian government refused to send his body to Canada, where his family lives.

March 4, 2004: Ardeshir Afshinzadeh, a twenty-five-year-old film editor, died of a brain hemorrhage after being beaten up by the Ansar-e Hezbollah. He had severe internal bleeding, and his liver was completely smashed. The Iranian State Security Forces claimed that he had jumped from a fifth story window, but there were no broken bones. Signs of torture were visible.

March 9, 2004: Answering a question about a prisoner who was flogged to death, GhollamHossein Elham, a spokesman for the Iranian Judiciary said, "What is the media looking for in this story? If something happens to someone in prison, is it due to actions opposing the law? It may be that someone becomes injured because of proper and legal punishments. Injuries come from the nature of the punishment, which is legal, not the crime and not the torture."[35] In other words, you can do what you want to them if you call it punishment rather than torture.

In April of 2004, Iran's chief justice, Ayatollah Shahroudi, banned the use of torture to obtain confessions[36]. It is unclear whether the ban applies to torture for other purposes, such as discouraging complaints, settling scores, or amusing sadistic prison employees.

The United Nations has been aware of the deplorable human rights situation in Iran and has issued reports and recommendations about it over the years. In some years UN inspectors have been allowed to enter Iran to investigate the human rights abuses, but in other years they have been kept out. The Iranian government does not

Three men hanged in public in Tehran.

care what the United Nations thinks, but is concerned about what it might do, particularly if any UN sanctions were threatened that could interfere with things it cares about, such as assistance with nuclear technology. So far the Khomeini outlaw regime has avoided the imposition of damaging UN sanctions, but it has not avoided adverse publicity.

In a resolution adopted on December 22, 2003, the United Nations General Assembly made the following remarks:

> However, the Assembly would express its serious concern at the continuing violations of human rights in Iran, the continued deterioration of the situation with regard to freedom of opinion and expression and the continuing executions in the absence of respect for internationally recognized safeguards. Concern would also be expressed at the use of torture and other forms of cruel punishment, in particular the practice of amputation and public executions, as well as the systeatic discrimination against women and girls in the law.[37]

Flogging is a common form of punishment in Iran today, along with stoning to death for adultery and the amputation of arms or

Payman Amini, who was hanged in public in Tehran. Before his death, he said, "We did not kill anybody. Why do we have to die? This country is full of criminals who are never punished for their crimes. Why are we being executed?"

fingers. According to Amnesty International, during 2003 alone there were at least four stonings, 197 floggings, and eleven amputations.[38]

Most executions are by hanging or firing squad, and the hangings are often conducted in public places so that as many people as possible can see them. Some deaths by flogging also occur.

This woman was buried in sand up to her armpits, then stoned to death. Government regulations specify the size of stones to be used, so that the victims do not die too quickly.

Many people in Europe and the United States would like to believe that the Iranian government "lightened up" on dissent after Khatami was elected in 1997. This is untrue. Khatami simply has a better understanding of public relations than some of his colleagues. Khatami tries to avoid public relations disasters, whereas some of the hardliners don't care.

A good example is the recent case of Hashem Aghajari, a college professor at the Tehran Teachers' Training University. He gave a speech in June of 2002 which supported the Shi'ite tradition of encouraging good faith disputes and discussions on religious teachings. During the speech he said, "People should not follow hard line interpretations of Islam blindly like monkeys."[39].

Professor Aghajari was prosecuted for blasphemy, tried, convicted, and sentenced to death. Hundreds of thousands of students demonstrated. The Supreme Court ordered a retrial.

The trial judge tried him again, convicted him again, and sentenced him to death for blasphemy again. The students demonstrated again, and the Supreme Court set aside the death sentence again. Khatami criticized the trial judge as "inexperienced."[40]

The prosecutors pushed for a third trial. This time Professor Aghajari was convicted of insulting Islamic principles and given a five-year sentence with three years actual jail time and two years suspended sentence[41]. On July 31, 2004, he was released on bail before serving the full three years[42].

Without the student demonstrations, Professor Aghajari would be a dead man.

Another example of internal terrorism by the Iranian government is the murder of an eighty-year-old man, Mohammad Reza Baharlou, in Darab, Iran, on October 22, 1998. He was vigorous, healthy, and well liked. But his son, Ahmed Reza Baharlou, is a producer of *Voice of America* TV shows that are broadcast into Iran in Farsi. Prior to Mr. Baharlou's murder, the son had interviewed an Iranian defector, the son of General Ahmad Rezai, a former commander of the Iranian Revolutionary Guard[43].

None of these abuses are necessary to rule a country and keep the peace. The fact that the mullahs, ayatollahs, and their backers have done it for twenty-five years is ample evidence that they are unfit to govern anything, let alone a nuclear power with more than sixty-eight million people. If they treat their own people this way, imagine what they would do to people of other countries if they ever get the chance.

It is time for the Iranian people to put them out of business, and for the United States and the other freedom-loving countries of the world to lend them whatever assistance and encouragement we can.

The audience reacton to the public hangings.

Chapter 6

The Lives of Women and Children in Iran

If you talk to Iranians coming from Iran, they will tell you that they are not living, merely existing. You may meet other people who have benefited from the mullahs, but most Iranians are desperately unhappy. In Iran, there is no freedom of speech, freedom of the press, or fun at the beach. Even at the beach, a woman's head must be fully covered, and her body must be covered from head to toe.

The chador, a shapeless black garment that covers the entire body, is mandatory for women, as is a head scarf concealing all the hair. Women with inadequate chadors or who allowed a few strands of hair to show from under a scarf are often beaten, mutilated, or even killed, depending on the whims of whoever saw them.

A woman wearing lipstick runs a serious risk of beatings or mutilation of the lips or face if the wrong people see her. Some people claim there has been improvement in the last few years[44], but now that the Majlis is stacked with Khomeini extremists, the trend is toward increasing restrictions, regulations, and brutality.

The Iranian Morality Police have now forbidden clothing stores from showing mannequins with lingerie. All mannequins must be veiled and wearing chadors, and men are now forbidden from working in stores that sell lingerie[45]. Sex change operations will still be legal though, as they were approved by Khomeini many years ago, and his fatwas cannot be reversed.

In July of 2004, Khamenei called for national clothing styles that are different from European clothes, and the Majlis is now discussing the enactment of a national dress code for men and women[46]. Western clothing would be banned altogether, and nobody would have the slightest degree of personal freedom.

Relations between the sexes are also heavily regulated. Women and men are kept apart as much as possible, and women are not allowed to appear in public with any men except male relatives. On days when the police (or unregulated private militia members) are bored and looking for easy fun, they may harass a woman even if she can prove the man with her is a son, nephew, husband, or uncle.

Dating and social activities between teenagers and young adults are strictly forbidden. Young Iranians try to get around this prohibition in low risk ways, such as gatherings in home and walks in national parks and mountains. The parks are patrolled by Morality Police, who often follow the couples, harass them, and try to prevent them from having a good time. The punishment is more severe if the couple is caught holding hands, kissing, or otherwise touching, but even non-sexual pleasure or enjoyment can provoke government sanctions.

The punishment can be heavy. In one instance, a college girl caught in public with a boy her own age was sentenced to ninety lashes with a whip, or a fine. She paid the fine[47]. Sometimes, the defendant is not given an option as to the form of punishment.

In March of 2000, police raided a dance party in a private home in Shiraz. They prosecuted forty-two young men and women, who each were sentenced to thirty-five lashes each. The homeowner was fined 100 million rials, about $12,300.[48].

The Iranian government also prohibits many kinds of entertainment that other people all over the world enjoy. Satellite TV, videos, liquor, dancing between couples of the opposite sex, modern music, and uncensored movies are all forbidden[49]. People have also been arrested for playing cards in their home[50].

Dancing is also illegal. Some forms of traditional dance and belly dancing are nonetheless allowed in private homes most of the time, but if the Morality Police are bored, restless, or insufficiently bribed, the dancers and audience can be arrested and severely punished for

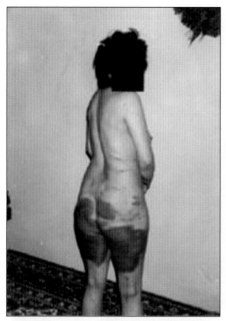

The Iranian government did this. She was not guilty of anything, so after beating her with metal cables, they let her go. They will kill her for being in this picture if they ever find out who she is.

violating public morals. This can result in the death penalty in extreme cases.

Sometimes the Iranian government arrests dancers and entertainers simply to intimidate the public and raise the general level of fear. The Iranian government will sometimes also murder entertainers outside the country, to "send a message." This has become less frequent since Khomeini's death in 1989, but the climate of fear still prevails. As a result, overseas Iranians have difficulty trusting each other. You never know when you might be talking to a spy who will report you to the Iranian government.

Even pets are regulated. Some Iranian clerics have called for the arrest of dog owners and their dogs, on the grounds that dogs are unclean under Islamic law[51]. They overlook the point that nothing can exist unless God wills it so, and that applies to dogs as much as anything else. In the meantime, they ignore more serious problems, such as prostitution, disease, teenage suicide, unemployment, resource degradation, overpopulation, and drug addiction.

Narcotics are plentiful in Iran[52], and more than two million Iranians use them every day[53]. It is estimated that more than sixty percent of the crime in Iran, and more than seventy percent of the AIDS cases, are drug-related[54]. The AIDS statistic is difficult to assess with confidence, because there is little or no reliable information on the extent of gay sex in Iran. The Khomeini government has frequently executed gay men, so gays and lesbians keep a very low profile.

73

Examples of Khomeini's dress code for women. The one in back is pushing the boundaries by revealing a dangerous amount of forehead, which could lead to the exposure of one or more strands of hair.

Prostitution is a major problem in Iran. It is estimated that Iran has more than 300,000 street prostitutes[55], with 84,000 in Tehran alone[56]. A nongovernmental, dissident Iranian cleric, Hojatolislam Hadi Ghabel, said, "Thirteen and fourteen-year-old junior high school girls now engage in prostitution, and I ask how can it be that under such degrading conditions the regime wastes billions of dollars on worthless programs . . . ?"[57]

Prostitution is illegal and can be punished by death, especially if accompanied by alcohol, partying, and enjoyment. In 1997 three women were stoned to death in Khazar Abad after being convicted of adultery and prostitution. The stoning was carried out by public-spirited local citizens[58]. Their male customers were also stoned to death, a rare case where both sexes received equal treatment.

In another incident, a husband and wife were executed for organizing "corrupt gatherings" with prostitutes, alcohol, drugs, music, and dance. An aggravating factor was the presence of Iranian political leaders at the event[59].

The death sentence is not mandatory, and there seems to be little consistency in sentencing from one case to another, In early 2003, a Jordanian newspaper reported that an Iranian court had sentenced ninety members of a prostitution ring to a total of 4,710 lashes and prison terms. The ring controlled twenty-four brothels[60].

Prostitution takes two forms in Iran, ordinary street prostitution and temporary marriage contracts, called sigeh. The terms of the sigeh are negotiated in great detail: when can the man come visit, how much does he pay each time, and when does the sigeh end. Every sigeh expires after a specific length of time, anywhere from one hour to ninety-nine years. The sigeh must be registered with the Iranian government to provide a complete defense to charges of prostitution[61]. The sigeh is not part of Persian culture but rather an innovation introduced by the Arabs when they invaded in the seventh century.

The sigeh is considered legitimate under Shi'ite Islamic tradition. In its pre-Islamic form among some Arab tribes, the woman continued living with her family and any resulting children belonged to her family rather than the man's[62]. This practice was probably beneficial for isolated groups of people living before the time of the Prophet Muhammad in the seventh century. By allowing men from elsewhere to reproduce with local women, it promoted genetic diversity and reduced the risk of inbreeding and genetic defects. At times when the male population was too low, due to warfare, it enabled tribes to increase their numbers more quickly. And it probably reduced the number of homicides over women and family honor.

The modern version of sigeh is somewhat different. The resulting children belong to the father's family, not the mother's. Sigeh became more common as "an urban function associated with long distance trade"[63] rather than for male visitors to remote desert tribes. Over the years other features have been added:

The woman's family cannot block the sigeh, whereas permanent marriages are often arranged without the woman's consent.

A man has no limit on the number of temporary wives, unlike the four-wife limit on permanent wives.

Whenever prostitution increases in a country, sexually transmitted disease rates increase soon after. This happened in Iran, and sigeh has played a part in the growing epidemic of sexually transmitted diseases. A study performed at the Kermanshah University of Medical Sciences involving 100 men with gonorrhea found that four percent became infected by girlfriends, twenty-four percent by sigeh wives, and sixty-four percent by street prostitutes[64]; the remaining eight percent denied having sex with either prostitutes or sigeh wives. The conclusions reached in the study are striking:

> The majority of the prostitutes and sigeh wives in Iran exchange sex for survival. Being uneducated survival sex workers, they accept risky sex behaviours easily. Sigeh wives are an important source of infection. The very high rate of persistent infection despite standard treatments is disturbing . . . Denying the presence of such realities as prostitution and sexually transmitted diseases (STDs) because of their disagreement with cant claims and official propaganda does not eradicate the facts but results in catastrophic public health problems.[65]

The problem of prostitution is also connected to homelessness. There are an estimated 1,700,000 homeless women in Iran[66], most of whom receive no welfare or support, and this contributes to the increase in prostitution.

In addition, there are more than one million homeless children in Iran[67]. Most of them work as street vendors, with forty-one percent of them selling drugs and thirty-seven percent of them addicted to drugs[68]. Other street children work as itinerant merchants, wash car windshields at red lights, beg for money, or shine the shoes of passers by[69]. A huge percentage of them have heart disease[70].

More than 23,500 children were rounded up off the streets of Tehran alone in an eleven-month period, according to the Welfare Organization of Tehran Province[71]. Although there are a few private charities working in this area, the number of children in need vastly outweighs their limited resources.

Child abuse is also a growing problem, with roughly 150 cases per day in the Iranian courts[72]. The actual number of cases is much greater, since most abusers manage to avoid being caught.

Some children from rural villages are sent to work in sweatshops, such as rug manufacturing facilities. Several of these are located in the city of Ghom, where children as young as seven have been brought and forced to work up to sixteen hours per day[73]. The Assistant Social Service Director of the Welfare Department of Ghom, Hojatolislam Val-Moslemin, has denied that there is a problem[74]. Other Iranian industries that use child labor include masonry, glass making, textiles, chemical production, auto repair, farming, mining, pottery, and construction[75].

Iran has child labor laws, but they are rarely enforced. A prominent Iranian lawyer, Shirin Ebadi, has summarized the problem this way:

> According to the law, working age is from fifteen to eighteen years. The working child is entitled to physical checkups, physician approval for suitability of work, no permission to work graveyard shifts, overtime, and the right to work thirty minutes less a day. These laws perhaps are the most progressive laws for young workers. In addition to labor laws, allowing equal pay for equal work, the young worker is under protection of social welfare. But these are all one side of the coin. The other side of the coin is the story of the families who cannot wait for their children to reach fifteen years of age to force them to work. In the illegal sweatshops that are managed by children now, no laws or security prevails and all of these sweatshops exist hidden away from the eyes of the Labor Ministry's investigators[76].

Oddly, current Iranian law does not have a standard age at which childhood ends. This is left up to a case-by-case determination, with absurd inconsistencies resulting[77].

As attorney Ebadi has pointed out, "Under the penal code, if a girl of nine and a boy of fifteen commit a crime, they are punished as adults . . . . However, if the same boy or girl participates in children's painting competition and wins, he/she needs to obtain the father's permission to receive passport for travel. Furthermore, . . . we see that the same boy or the girl cannot participate in the elections as a voter. On the other hand, a lady at the age of forty, who . . . wants to marry for the first time, needs her father's permission to do so"[78].

The Iranian criminal laws of the 1920s, which were also Islamic, were actually more sensible and compassionate than the current laws. Under the former laws, children under age six did not have the legal capacity to commit crimes and were therefore not punished. Children from ages six to twelve were deemed to know right from wrong and would receive a mild punishment. For children between twelve and eighteen the punishments were gradually increased in severity as their mental and moral capabilities grew. For example, a child under eighteen who committed a murder could receive up to five years in jail[79].

Of course, any woman or child who offends a Khomeini outlaw regime judge could receive the death sentence, regardless of what they are charged with. That happened recently to a sixteen-year old rape victim who was brought into court in northern Iran for "acts incompatible with chastity."

The girl, Atefeh Sahaleh aka Atefeh Rajabi, did not have a lawyer, and the judge would not grant her a continuance to get one[80]. During the trial, the judge criticized her appearance. She became enraged, took off some part of her clothing[81], and castigated him. She told him that he should be punishing the perpetrators of crime, not its victims[82].

Atefeh's male co-defendant, the rapist, received a sentence of 100 lashes[83], but Atefeh was sentenced to death.

Under current Iranian law, death sentences must be approved by the Supreme Court of the Islamic Republic before they are carried out. Judge Reza ran the case through the system at top speed and got Supreme Court approval in only three months. No papers were filed by Atefeh, nor were any hearings held before the Supreme Court. Her father's efforts to get a lawyer for her ended in failure; no lawyer would take her case.

On August 15, 2004, Atefeh was executed by public hanging from a crane. Judge Haji Reza personally put the rope around her neck and ordered the crane operator to begin lifting[84]. He rejoiced in the killing and announced that she had not been executed for her crime but for her "sharp tongue."[85].

We do not know whether Atefeh was raped before Haji Reza executed her, but it appears likely. Somebody stole Atefeh's corpse from her grave the night she was buried[86]. It is hard to think of a rational reason why anyone would do this, except to prevent a forensic examination for evidence of rape or torture.

The Khomeini fatwa requiring the rape of all virgins before executing them did not apply to Atefeh, since her crime (being a rape victim) resulted in the loss of her virginity prior to trial.

Atefeh's family called for an investigation, but Haji Reza is the chief judge for the province of Mazandaran. The likelihood that anything will happen is minimal. The parents have no legal recourse for their daughter's death.

It is difficult for decent people to understand how any legitimate government could sentence someone to death for contempt of court. It is equally difficult to understand how any real supreme court judge could complete a death penalty appeal in three months with no briefs filed and no legal representation for the defendant. Denying a defendant a continuance in a death penalty case in order to find a lawyer is also difficult to understand.

It is worth noting that long before Atefeh's trial, Iran signed an international convention forbidding the execution of people before they turn eighteen. Apparently international treaties are not binding law in Judge Reza's courtroom.

Haji Reza is an extreme case, but he is not the only mullah with a harsh attitude toward women and girls. Most Khomeini outlaw regime insiders have negative attitudes toward women. Rafsanjani has said what many of them secretly think:

> The difference in the stature, vitality, voice, development, muscular quality, and physical strength of men and women show that men are stronger and more capable in all fields. Men's brains are bigger so men are more inclined to fight and women are more excitable. Men are inclined to reasoning and rationalism, while women have a fundamental tendency to be emotional. The tendency to protect is stronger in men . . . Such differences affect the delegation of responsibilities, duties, and rights[87].

At least three other Iranian Ayatollahs have expressed similar low opinions of women.

"The specific task of women in this society is to marry and bear children. They will be discouraged from entering legislative, judicial, or whatever careers which may require decision making, as women lack the intellectual ability and discerning judgment required for theses careers."— Ayatollah Mutahari[88]

"Most Europeans have mistresses. Why should we suppress human instincts? A rooster satisfies several hens, a stallion several mares. A woman is unavailable during certain periods whereas a man is always active . . . ,"— Ayatollah Ghomi, *LE MONDE,* January 20, 1979[89].

"A woman becomes available to a man in three ways: permanent matrimony, temporary nuptials, and slavery."[90].— Ayatollah Ali Meshkini, chairman of the Assembly of Experts

"Depravity comes with three things: women, animals, and houses."[91].— Also Ayatollah Meshkini.

Some of these ayatollahs doubtless share Khomeini's belief that raping virgin female prisoners before they are executed is a desirable social policy. Khomeini issued a fatwa requiring this, truly an obscene blot on the face of Islam. The reasoning behind it will astonish civilized people.

The starting point is the "problem" that virgins can be condemned to death but will go to heaven if they are actually executed. This state of affairs is intolerable, but it is equally intolerable to let them live after committing capital crimes, such as blasphemy or talking back to Judge Reza.

The Khomeini outlaw solution is to require women's jailers to rape them, so that they are not virgins when they die. Under Khomeini's logic, rape is equated with voluntary sex. Once the virgins have been raped, they will go to hell and it is safe to kill them[92]. Khomeini's clerics laugh at the notion that God might be displeased with their efforts to prevent women from going to heaven.

Khomeini's fatwas cannot be revoked by a subsequent supreme leader, or so they claim. This means that the only way to stop the raping of female prisoners is to destroy the Khomeini outlaw regime and replace it with a new government that repudiates Khomeini's fatwas and prosecutes anyone carrying them out.

Some Americans wonder why the decent, God-loving clerics in other Islamic countries seldom, if ever, denounce this sort of thing. One possibility is that they do but that their denunciations rarely get coverage in the American media.

A more convincing theory is that Iran's ties to various terrorist groups make it easy to murder critics anywhere in the Moslem world. Experience has convinced the Iranian government that if they plan carefully and deny everything, they can commit murder without any serious consequences.

There are other inequalities between the sexes. Iranian men may marry foreign women, but Iranian women cannot marry foreign men without a government permit.

Married women are not allowed to leave Iran without a written permission slip from their husbands, and even then they sometimes have more difficulty than men attempting to leave. At the same time, women are allowed to go to college and are expected to constitute the majority of college graduates in a few years. This could mean trouble for the Khomeini outlaw regime.

The Iranian college faculty and curriculum are different from those in America and Europe. Marxism, communism, and their derivatives are not taught in a favorable light, but the mere process of attending college and learning to think in that manner is likely to lead to increasing discontent with dress codes and sexual discrimination.

Chapter 7

Khatami's Iran: Home Base for Terrorists

Governments that behave like the Khomeini outlaw regime are a threat to other governments and other people. The threat which Iran poses has been seen clearly by American presidents of both parties. On November 14, 1979, the tenth day of the Iranian hostage crisis, President Carter declared a state of emergency with respect to Iran in Executive Order 12170. This order has been renewed by every president since then and is still in effect[93].

On March 15, 1995, President Clinton declared another national emergency[94]. He found Iran to be an unusual and extraordinary threat to the national security, foreign policy, and economy of the United States, based on

1. its support for international terrorism,

2. its efforts to undermine the Middle East peace process, and

3. its acquisition of missiles and weapons of mass destruction

In 2004, President Bush found that President Clinton's 1995 declaration of emergency was still appropriate and continued his executive order in force[95]. The state of emergency is not likely to end any time soon.

The election of Mohammad Khatami as president of Iran did not reduce the danger. Many people had hoped it would, but it had no impact on the Iranian government's support of worldwide terrorism or its planning and scheming to destroy the governments, economies, and civilizations of North America, South America, Israel, and Europe. Khatami hasn't slowed down the hardliners at all. In fact, he helped speed up their nuclear weapons program by replacing incompetent mullahs with physicists and engineers.

The mullahs had viewed the program as a prestigious and profitable sinecure, and they were naturally in no hurry to see it end. Khatami replaced these political hacks with qualified nuclear scientists and engineers, and the program sped up remarkably. Now they are only one or two years away from making their first atomic bomb[96].

It is important to remember that Khatami is a Khomeini insider just like the rest of them. Before the 1979 revolution, he spent many years of his life preparing, duplicating, and distributing Khomeini's political statements. He worked hard to advance Khomeini's cause, and he knew Khomeini personally. In college he worked closely with Khomeini's late son, Hojatolislam Ahmad Khomeini.

Khomeini appointed him the head of the Kayhan Institute in 1981, and during the Iran-Iraq War he also served in the military and as chairman of the War Propaganda Headquarters[97]. When the war ended, he became the Director of Ideological and Cultural Affairs. He continued to enthusiastically support Khomeini even after he ordered the execution of more than 8,000 prisoners[98].

It is not surprising that Khatami appeals more to Americans, Europeans, women, and college students than his colleagues. He understands public relations and knows how to tell people what they want to hear.

The hardliners in the Khomeini outlaw regime do not care whether they are liked, as long as they are feared. The only thing that really adversely affects them is a major drop in the price of oil. That reduces the amount of money they can spend buying weapons and financing terrorism. The bombing, killing, torture, and maiming do not stop, but the number of terrorist attacks goes down.

The behavior of the Iranian government did not improve after Khatami was elected. One Iranian opposition group, the Mujahedeen Khalq, claimed that during Khatami's first year as president of Iran,

There were 260 public hangings.

The Khobar Towers complex in Saudi Arabia

Hundreds of political prisoners were secretly executed.

Seven people were stoned to death.

Jailers used more than 170 different forms of torture on prisoners.

Twenty-eight Iranian dissidents were assassinated abroad.

Fourteen terrorist attacks, including car bombs and mortar attacks, were made on Iranian resistance members.

Terrorist groups in Arab countries were paid 270 million dollars.[99]

Under Khatami, the Iranian government is still financing terrorism worldwide. They usually hire other people to do the atrocities, while they plan and finance them from behind the scenes. They have maximum impact with minimum accountability. This pattern has occurred in incidents both before and after Khatami's first term in office.

Good examples of pre-Khatami terrorism include the killing of four Kurdish dissidents in the Mykonos Restaurant in Berlin in 1992, the Khobar Towers bombing in 1996, and the bombing of a Jewish community center in Buenos Aires, Argentina, in 1994.

The bomb crater at the Khobar Towers complex

Iran's involvement in the Argentine attack was more obvious than usual. Four of the five main terrorists were Iranians, and the fifth, Imad Mugniyeh, lived in Iran. The explosives were bought from Colombian drug dealers and transported by the Islamic Republic of Iran Shipping Lines. One of the five main men, Ali Fallahian, was a key intelligence adviser to Khamenei[100]. Other conspirators in the bombing included Mohsen Rabhani, an attaché at the Iranian Embassy in Argentina, and Hamid Naghasan, a senior Iranian intelligence officer. The ambassador, Hadi Soleimanpour, was probably in on it also[101].

Soleimanpour was withdrawn from Argentina shortly after the bombing[102], and the Argentine government had to wait nine years before they could even try to extradite him for questioning. They got their chance in 2003, when he entered Great Britain to take classes at Durham University[103]. An Interpol arrest warrant was issued, and the British Police picked him up on August 21, 2003[104]. Khatami was enraged by this and demanded that the British let him go. The government that broke the rule of diplomatic immunity in 1979 was outraged when someone else arrested one of their former diplomats.

FBI photo of Imad Mugniyeh on its most wanted list.

The British held Soleimanpour in custody for several months pending the extradition hearing. On November 12, 2003, Argentina's extradition request was denied on the grounds of insufficient evidence. A week later he flew back to Iran. So far this extradition proceeding is the only time Soleimanpour has spent in jail for the murder of eighty-five people.

After blowing up the community center, the Iranians tried to sabotage the police investigation. Evidence disappeared, investigators were harassed, and witnesses were intimidated. The most spectacular part of the cover-up was a $10,000,000 bribe to the president of Argentina. He continued in office until 1999. When the bribe was discovered, he denied it and complained about bias against Moslems.

Many of the details of the bombing conspiracy were first disclosed by Abdolghassem Mesbahi, an Iranian government official who defected to Germany in 1996. He did not defect because of the bombing but because he felt too many dissident intellectuals were being murdered by the Iranian government.

Between 1979 and 2000, Tehran's agents murdered forty-six Iranians, seventeen of them in France, and killed more than eighty non-Iranians in various terrorist operations in the European Union. On each occasion, the European country involved made some angry noises, and, in some cases, gestures such as closing the embassy and recalling the ambassador. In the end, however, they all ended up eating humble pie served by at the hand of the triumphant mullahs.[105]

Mr. Mesbahi's attitude is common among ordinary Iranians, who feel that vigorous political debate is healthy and that free speech should be protected. For the Iranians, this attitude comes from the Shi'ite branch of Islam as well as Zoroastrianism. Under the Shi'ite tradition, vigorous arguments and questioning of established views are considered desirable, as long as they do not cross the line into heresy, idolatry, or blasphemy. From this point of view, the torture and killing of dissenters and critics is un-Islamic, a crime against God, and an impediment to the moral evolution of the human race. Many other Iranians in Mesbahi's position would have done the same thing, and this is one of the reasons the Khomeini outlaw regime is ripe for overthrow and replacement by a democracy. Khatami's election as president did not change the Iranian government's terrorism campaign against Americans. There is little difference between what they did in 1996, before the election, and 1998, after Khatami was in office.

The Khobar Towers bombing in Saudi Arabia was the worst Iranian act of terrorism against Americans in 1996. The Iranians tried to conceal their involvement, but by November of 1998, FBI Director Louis Freeh had evidence that Khamenei had asked an Iranian brigadier general to target the Khobar Towers[106].

The actual bombing was done by Hezbollah[107]. This delayed the FBI's discovery of Khamenei's role for about two years. The Clinton administration investigated the bombing for another two years without filing any criminal proceedings[108]. The Bush administration followed up by filing a criminal indictment charging thirteen defendants with the murders of nineteen American servicemen[109]. The 9/11 Commission believes that al Qaeda collaborated with Iran and Hezbollah, but has not stated exactly what al Qaeda did to further the attack[110].

Iran was also behind the 1983 bombing of a United States Marine barracks in Beirut, Lebanon, that killed 241 American servicemen. Iran ordered and financed the bombing and sent one of their top terrorist organizers, Feridoun Mehdi-Nezhad, to meet with Hezbollah in Lebanon to plan it. After the bombing the Iranian government paid Hezbollah the agreed fee for its services.

Not all of the details of payment are known, but the hiring of Hezbollah to do the bombing was established by proof in a court of law that followed rigorous evidentiary procedures, including the right of cross examination of witnesses. In May of 2003, United States District Court Judge Royce Lambirth, ruled that the bombing was financed by the Iranian Ministry of Information and Security. He further found the attack was approved by Khamenei and Rafsanjani and could not have been carried out without their approval[111].

The key figure in this attack was Imad Mugniyeh, a Lebanese-born terrorist who joined Hezbollah in 1983. He reported directly to Ali Akbar Mohtashemipour, an Iranian ambassador and exporter of terrorism, homicide, death, and destruction.

Mugniyeh has frequently directed the kidnapping, torturing, and killing Americans and has been credited with:

The bombing of the United States Embassy in Beirut in 1983 (sixty-three deaths)

The bombing of the United States Marine barracks in Lebanon in 1983 (241 brave American Marines and fifty-eight French soldiers died)

The hijacking of TWA Flight 847 from Greece to Beirut in 1985 and the torture and murder of passenger Robert Stethem, a United States Navy diver, whose body was dumped onto an airport runway

The hijacking of a Kuwait Airlines flight in 1988, followed by the torture and murder of two Kuwaiti passengers and the dumping of their bodies onto an airport runway

The 1992 bombing of the Israeli embassy in Argentina (twenty-nine deaths)

An unsuccessful 1996 attempt to bomb an El Al airplane (the explosives went off before the bomber left his hotel)

Meetings with Osama bin Laden going back to 1993

Meetings between 2000 and 2002 with Iraqi intelligence officers, bin Laden, and bin Laden's deputy, Ayman al-Zawahiri.[112]

The kidnapping, torture, and murder of CIA station chief William Buckley in 1984. Buckley's story is a tragic one. Before joining the CIA, he served as a Lieutenant Colonel in the U. S. Army during the Vietnam War. At the time of his kidnapping in March 1984, he was the senior CIA representative in Lebanon. His kidnappers called themselves the "Islamic Holy War" to disguised their true identity: Hezbollah, backed and funded by the Iranian government. He

Lt. Colonel William Buckley during the Vietnam War

remained missing for seven years, and there is good reason to believe that he was imprisoned in Iran for part of that time. In 1991 his skull and a few bones were found wrapped in a blanket near the Beirut airport and identified by Lebanese and American forensic specialists. His remains were returned to the United States in December of 1991, and he was buried with full honors at Arlington National Cemetary. The awards he received during his lifetime include the Bronze Star with V, Silver Star, two Purple Hearts, Combat Infantry Badge, Parachutist's Badge, Meritorious Service Medal, and several CIA awards, including the Intelligence Star, Exceptional Service Medallion, and Distinguished Intelligence Cross.

His days in captivity in Lebanon were particularly heart-rending, according to one of his cellmates, David Jacobsen.

> "One of the chilling moments for me and for Terry Anderson was to hear Bill Buckley cough," says Jacobson.
>
> He was very sick. He was delirious. I heard him say, "I don't know what happened to my body; it was so strong thirty days ago.' "[113]

William Buckley less than a year before his kidnapping and murder.

This may have been Colonel Buckley's way of letting his cellmates know how long he had been there, so that they could tell others if they were released. The Hezbollah prisoners were not allowed to talk with each other, so by appearing delirious and talking to no one in particular, he may have avoided punishment. He never gave up, and even in extreme sickness his mind was sharp.

More than thirteen years after Colonel Buckley was buried, Imad Mugniyeh is still on the FBI's most wanted list. The FBI web site states their belief that Mugniyeh is in Lebanon, but in fact he is married to an Iranian woman and lives in Iran.

United States agents have spotted Mugniyeh twice after Buckley's death, once in France in 1986 and again in Saudi Arabia in 1995. Unfortunately, the French and Saudi governments turned down American requests to arrest him. They deliberately let him get away. The French did not seem to care that he caused the deaths of fifty-eight of their soldiers and 241 of ours.

The Iranian government's involvement in the crimes of Mugniyeh goes beyond moral support. They were his bankers. Without their financial support, none of his atrocities would have been possible, in the opinion of Israeli security expert Shimon Shapira, who told a reporter, "This man isn't working alone. All his power comes from his reliance on the Iranian intelligence service. None of his operations could have been executed without their infrastructure. This infrastructure is very wide, ranging from embassies [and] commerce delegations to all other Iranian state activities."[114]

Some people think that Mugniyeh may now be in Iraq, trying to kill Americans. It seems unlikely the Iranian government would desire this, because he is a key liaison to al Qaeda and would be hard to replace if he were killed. It makes more sense to let him plan the evil deeds, then hire men from starving families to carry them out. The level of unemployment and despair in the Middle East is so high that men can always be found who will drive a truck filled with explosives into a building, so that their wives and children will have a decent place to live and enough to eat.

There is another reason to doubt the rumors that Imad Mugniyeh is in Iraq. That would be out of character for him, because soldiers can fight back. Normally he selects victims who cannot resist. It would take courage for him to go into battle against American soldiers, and he has not shown much of that in his career, only cunning and depravity.

The Iranian government does not use the same people for every terrorist atrocity it commits. For example, Imad Mugniyeh was not involved in the explosion of Pan Am Flight 103 over Scotland on December 21, 1988. This terrorist incident has been blamed on Libyans and the Libyan government, but it was the Iranian government which ordered the bombing and paid to have it carried out in a way that would conceal their involvement.

The Iranian government followed the same procedure it had used in ordering and financing the bombing of the U. S. Embassy in Beirut in 1983. A local terrorist group was selected, then an Iranian agent met with them. The locals agreed to do the dirty work, a price was negotiated, and after the attack they were paid in full by the Iranian government.

The wheels were set in motion when Feridoun Mehdi-Nezhat, a Pasdaran (Iranian Revolutionary Guard) member, went to the Damur refugee camp in Lebanon to meet with two representatives of the Popular Front for the Liberation of Palestine/General Command, a group skilled in sophisticated bombing attacks. One of the men, Muhammad Dalqamuni, had done favors for Iran in the past, while the other man, Nabil Makhzumi, spoke Farsi and was the group's main liaison with the Iranian Revolutionary Guard.

Mehdi-Nezhat told them that the Iranian government wanted to bomb an American plane in mid-flight with maximum casualties, the more the better. The General Command agreed to do the job and chose Pan Am Flight 103 as the target. They coordinated the attack with terrorists in Germany, Libya, and elsewhere. It was planned so well that on the day Pan Am 103 went down, Dalqamuni was in police custody in Germany. Dalqamuni was caught in a police roundup, but as former CIA case officer Robert Baer[115] has pointed out, his associate Muhammad Abu Talib, was not caught and could have carried it out. This is almost certainly what happened; there is no other plausible explanation for why Abu Talib received $500,000 four months after the incident.

The General Command received its $11 million fee two days after Flight 103 went down. The money was deposited in a Swiss bank account, then moved to a French bank and finally the Hungarian Trade Development Bank. Dalqamuni had the French bank account number prior to the attack on Flight 103. It was on his person when the Germans arrested him in October of 1988.

Eventually two Libyans were prosecuted for the act, and the Libyan government was also blamed for it. But the Iranian government set the wheels in motion, by ordering the crime and then paying for it.

The Iranian agent, Feridoun Mehdi-Nezhad, has been involved in many terrorist activities besides Flight 103 and the 1983 Beirut embassy bombing. His activities include Imad Mugniyeh's hijacking of Flight 847, the Khobar Towers bombing, and the negotiations that freed French hostages in 1987 and American hostages in 1991. He is a major figure in the Iranian government terror apparatus, and as of 2002 he was a political ally of Khatami[116]. This is further evidence that Khatami is no different than Khamenei or Rafsanjani when it comes to terrorism against the United States.

One of the things the Khomeini outlaw regime does is to play off its enemies against each other. By keeping the Europeans angry at the Americans, they hope to prevent them from uniting against Iran. European intelligentsia and the legacy media in both the United States and Europe tend to be unwitting accomplices in this, by promoting hostility and differences. This rarely fools Europe's leaders but often creates political moods that they must deal with in taking public positions on policy issues.

In 1998 the Iranian government made up for lost time with simultaneous bombings of two United States Embassies, in Kenya and

Tanzania. The Kenya bombing (213 killed, 5000 injured) was more spectacular than the Tanzania bombing (ten killed, seventy injured). As usual, the Iranian government concealed its involvement in the attacks, which were initially blamed only on al Qaeda.

The most spectacular Iranian government terrorist attack during Khatami's presidency, in conjunction with al Qaeda, will almost certainly be the destruction of the World Trade Center in New York on September 11, 2001[117]. It would be difficult to find more convincing proof that Khatami has had no effect on Iran's resolutely anti-American foreign policy. Even Lajevardi, the Butcher of Evin Prison, never killed 3,000 people in one day.

But before condemning the Iranian government for 9/11, the evidence that it was actually involved must be examined.

Chapter 8

Iran, al Qaeda, and 9/11

After the 9/11 attack many Americans wondered whether Hezbollah was involved. This was a legitimate question, given their expertise in bombing and their attacks on the U. S. Embassy, Consulate, and Marine barracks in Lebanon in 1983. However, Hezbollah has not attacked the United States as often as al Qaeda in recent years. This point was made by Larry A. Mefford, the Assistant Director of the Counterterrorism Division of the FBI, in a statement to Congress on June 27, 2003. In his opinion al Qaeda has mounted at least twelve terrorist attacks against the United States and its allies since September 11, 2001[118]. These included three simultaneous attacks in Riyadh, Saudi Arabia, and five simultaneous bombings in Casablanca, all in 2003.

Most people agree that the 9/11 attack was carried out by al Qaeda[119]. Al Qaeda's best-known spokesman, Osama bin Laden, admitted this in a videotape that was distributed world-wide in 2004.

For some scholars and commentators, the involvement of al Qaeda automatically ruled out Iran as a suspect. These people held the opinion that Iran and al Qaeda could not possibly work together, due to their ideological and religious differences. Experience has shown that this was wishful thinking. Al Qaeda and the Iranian government have joined forces to attack, demoralize, and ultimately conquer America, Europe, and the West. Each of them doubtless intends to attack the other one after these shared goals are achieved, but in the meantime they are working together against America, Europe, and the oil-producing countries of the Middle East.

There is convincing evidence of Iran-al Qaeda cooperation during the 1990s, such as:

In 1995, Mustafa Hamid, an Egyptian al Qaeda member, visited Tehran.

In the early 1990s, meetings took place between Imad Mugniyeh, then living in Iran, and Osama bin Laden.

Ayman al-Zawahiri, a major al Qaeda operative, traveled to Iran several times in the 1990s. He already had Iranian connections through his membership in the Islamic Jihad of Egypt.

During 1997 and 1998, ten percent of Osama bin Laden's long distance phone calls were to numbers in Iran.[120]

Meetings of the leaders of both sides were arranged in the 1990s by Imad Mugniyeh and Ayman al Zawahiri.

Each side has found something in the other to admire. Iran was impressed by al Qaeda's attack on the U.S.S. Cole in Yemen[121], while al Qaeda could not help admiring Iran for killing so many Saudi Arabian intelligence officers.

The leaders on both sides agreed that Iran and al Qaeda should find targets they both wanted to attack. The World Trade Center in New York City was just such a target, and this is doubtless one of the reasons why the 9/11 conspiracy came into being.

During the years between their first meetings and the 9/11 attack, Iran and al Qaeda cooperated in a number of other activities, such as the training of al Qaeda members, money laundering, limited financial assistance, and forged documents. Iran also provided safe passage for al Qaeda operatives to and from Afghanistan. This was helpful to them, because several al Qaeda members had been arrested in airports in Pakistan, including Ramzi Yousef (1993 World Trade Center bombing) and Mir Amal Kansi (shooting of CIA employees at Langley, VA headquarters)[122]. By sending the terrorists into Afghanistan from Iran rather than Pakistan, al Qaeda avoided further arrests.

But none of Iran's earlier projects with al Qaeda can match the World Trade Center attack on September 11, 2001. Iran's role has not yet been established with absolute certainty, but there is both circumstantial and direct evidence that Iran planned and financed it and al Qaeda carried it out.

About one week before the September 11 attacks, Iran suddenly shut down the al Qaeda transit route to Afghanistan and wouldn't let any terrorists through. United States officials view this as circumstantial evidence that the Iranian government knew a major attack against the United States was coming and did not want any trails leading back to Iran. Before then, at least eight of the fourteen 9/11 hijackers had already passed through Iran[123].

Direct evidence consists of testimony by an Iranian defector, Hamid Reza Zakeri. He testified that Khamenei and Rafsanjani met in Tehran with bin Laden's son, Saad bin Laden, in May of 2001. Three other Khomeini outlaw regime ayatollahs were also present: Mohammed Yazdi, Ali Meshkini, and Mahdavi Kani[124].

Mr. Zakeri saw them arrive because he was in charge of the security for the meeting. He believes that this was when the final plans for 9/11 were drawn up. Shortly after the meeting, a display was set up in the entry hall of the Ministry of Information and Security. The display featured a missile with "Death to America" written on it in Arabic. Underneath the missile were models of the White House, the Pentagon, the World Trade Center, and Camp David[125]. This was put up before September 11, 2001, but it was only after the 9/11 attacks that the lower level Iranian government employees understood what it meant.

The meeting resulted in a memo dated May 14, 2001, from Ayatollah Nateq-Nouri to Hojatolislam Mustafa Pourghanadi (Ministry of Information and Security) to "improve our plans, especially in coordination with fighters of al Qaeda and Hezbollah to find one objective that is beneficial to both sides."[126] The memo also instructed Pourghanadi to deal with only two al Qaeda representatives, Imad Mugniyeh and Ayman al Zawahiri.

It is interesting that Khatami was not present at the May 4 meeting with al Qaeda. It may be that Khatami is simply not powerful enough to be consulted on terrorist activities. Khamenei and Rafsanjani are the most powerful men in the Iranian government and will always out-rank Khatami, regardless of what offices anyone is holding.

An additional reason not to have Khatami at the meeting might have been to maintain plausible deniability. If the United States dis-covered the truth and reacted with hostility, Khatami could truthfully deny any knowledge of it, claim the 9/11 plot was the work of irre-sponsible underlings, and promise to punish the offenders.

We cannot be absolutely certain that Mr. Zakeri's story is true. However, one commentator, Kenneth Timmerman, has obtained in-dependent corroboration that his description of the layout at the Min-istry of Information and Security is accurate. In addition, German prosecutors found his testimony persuasive enough to request a thirty-day continuance of the trial of Abdelghani Mzoudi, an alleged participant in the 9-11 conspiracy[127]. They hoped Zakeri would save their case, but in the end Mzoudi went free.

Mr. Zakeri's courtroom testimony included a statement that one of the 9/11 hijackers, Ziad Samir al-Jarrah, met in Iran with Imad Mugniyeh and Saef al-Adil, a top al Qaeda operative, two years before the 9/11 attack. He also testified that Mr. Mzoudi, the defendant, re-ceived terrorist training in Iran in 1997[128].

Ultimately Mzoudi was acquitted on the grounds of insufficient evidence[129]. Zakeri's testimony simply was not enough to convict Mzoudi. It was offset by a signed declaration from Ramzi Binalshibh that Mzoudi did not know about the 9/11 conspiracy. Mr. Binalshibh did not attend the trial, as he was unable to leave his residence at Guantanamo Bay.

There is additional circumstantial evidence tying Iran to the 9/11 attacks. Two of the hijackers stayed at the home of the Iranian ambas-sador to Malaysia prior to entering the United States in January 2001[130]. The hijackers, Nawaf al-Hamzi and Khalid al-Mihdhar, were not the sort of men one would expect to be traveling to exotic places or staying at the homes of ambassadors. Normally a senior diplomat would not give them the time of day. Obviously there was something special about these men that interested the Iranian ambassador, and we can reasonably assume that it had something to do with terrorism, death, and destruction.

It seems likely that additional corroborative evidence will appear in the future. Hopefully the internal files of the Iranian government will one day be released for public viewing, after the mullahs are out of office and the Khomeini outlaw regime has been destroyed. They are so proud of their crimes against God and humanity that they are almost certain to leave written records.

Chapter 9

Iran's Secret War in Iraq

Iran's mullahs were frightened when the United States invaded Iraq. They were pleased to see Saddam Hussein gone but upset at the increased American influence in the region. They have been trying to drive the United States out of the Middle East for many years, and they decided it was time to try harder. They took advantage of a Shi'ite holy day to send over 1,000 agents into Iraq. The spies, agitators, and subversives stayed behind after the ordinary Iranian citizens went home. Soon after that, terrorists and unemployed remnants of Saddam's forces began attacking American troops and Iraqi police with regularity. Some of the Iranian agents, including Revolutionary Guard troops, have been captured, along with munitions and military supplies manufactured in Iran. The forces of terror are well-funded, not only from Iran but also from Saddam's daughters, who took truckloads of wealth out of Iraq before his government fell.

The Iranian government still has Khomeini's dream of conquering not only Iraq but all of the Middle East. They think that Iraq could be taken over by subversion if the Americans left, and they may be right. Regionalism and tribalism are strong forces in Iraq, and the country could break into many small pieces if nobody holds it together. Iran's chances of gobbling up the pieces would be good if the United States did not interfere.

When the Saudi oil reserves start running low, anyone who controlled the oil in both Iraq and Iran could dominate world oil markets.

If they also had nuclear missiles, it would be very difficult for customers to get price reductions by threatening the use of force.

In addition, the Iranian government fears the growth of democracy in Afghanistan, Iraq, and Pakistan. If these countries succeed in establishing Islamic democracies, the Iranian people will have proof that it can be done and will be more inclined to fight for it. Democracy is actually more compatible with Islam than Khomeini's form of government, which has strong but concealed roots in fascism and communism.

During the earlier United States campaign in Afghanistan, the Iranian government sent in soldiers to help Taliban and al Qaeda members escape into Iran. Today thousands of these terrorists still live in Khorasan province. They can be armed and transported to Afghanistan on short notice. The railroad goes all the way to the Afghani border and beyond.

Iran's efforts to sabotage the United States in Afghanistan were not good karma. In 2002, a plane full of Revolutionary Guard soldiers took off for Afghanistan and almost immediately caught fire. Fortunately for them, the pilot was able to make an emergency landing[131].

In February of 2003, they were not so lucky. More than 280 Revolutionary Guard soldiers died when a plane returning from Afghanistan to Iran flew into a mountain [132]. For those who are superstitious and believe in "signs," the message was clear: Allah did not want the Revolutionary Guard making trouble in Afghanistan. Superstitious people are plentiful throughout the Middle East, but most of them are too sensible to share such views with the Iranian government, which reacts harshly to any suggestions that God is not on their side.

At any rate, Iran is proceeding full speed ahead with its secret Iraqi campaign against the United States. The al Qaeda forces are also involved and have been spotted moving supplies and fighters from Iran into Iraq[133]. They finally found a big project to work on with the Iranian government, it seems. Hopefully both terrorist groups will overplay their hands and be destroyed by Iraqi security forces.

One of the most visible Iranian agents in Iraq is Hojatolislam Muqtada al Sadr, an Iraqi Shi'ite cleric who has repeatedly ordered his followers to attack American troops[134]. His popularity is based on his father, who was a popular ayatollah until Saddam Hussein had him killed in 1999. Al Sadr is not bright enough to be an independent leader, which helps to make him an ideal Iranian government agent.

In July of 2003, al Sadr was already forming a "religious army" and calling for people to "fight the American and British occupiers," claiming that his army would use only "peaceful means"[135]. He dropped the peaceful means language in 2004, presumably after receiving weapons and ammunition from the Khomeini outlaw regime.

In April of 2004, the Iranian Ayatollah Kadhim Husseini al-Hairi (also spelled al-Haeri), who lives in Qom, made al Sadr his deputy in Iraq[136].

On June 4, 2004, al Sadr went to Iran to help celebrate the fourteenth anniversary of Khomeini's death. This is strange behavior for an Iraqi. Most Iraqis hate Khomeini for rejecting Saddam Hussein's settlement proposals and prolonging the Iraq-Iran War by six years. Khomeini's irrational stubbornness caused many needless Iraqi deaths.

During his visit, al Sadr met with Supreme Leader Khamenei and other top officials[137] who would normally not pay much attention to a hojatolislam from out of town. After al Sadr's return to Iraq:

pictures of Khomeini began appearing in Sadr City,

pro-Iranian activists were given more power and authority in his organization,

he occupied a major Islamic shrine and adjoining graveyard, and fought American and Iraqi troops for weeks,

Iraqi troops captured a grenade launcher marked "Made in Iran" from al Sadr troops, and

mortar shells falling on Iraqi homes had Iranian labels[138]

The shootout in the shrine ended when Iraq's number one Shi'ite cleric, Ayatollah Sistani, led thousands of Shi'ites there and brokered a settlement. A number of the marchers were killed along the way by mortar attacks from al Sadr supporters, but in the end al Sadr backed down and Sistani prevailed.

Sistani is a traditional Shi'ite cleric who rejects Khomeini's Supreme Leader concept and advocates the separation of church and state. He is a natural target for murder by the Iranian government, though they may wait until al Sadr is promoted to ayatollah before they try to kill Sistani. Several other Iraqi ayatollahs who opposed Khomeini's teachings have already been murdered. Hopefully Sistani will escape the Iranian government killers and help convince the Islamic world that Khomeini's doctrines should be discarded in the trash cans of history.

The Iranian government has never apologized for al Sadr's activities nor for its other acts of terrorism against America. Instead, it denies them when talking to Westerners and brags about them when talking to other terrorists. These deceits are often successful in causing confusion, disagreement, and passivity among their victims.

Victims are often afraid to retaliate against Iran for a particular terrorist act, in case they were not actually involved in it. This weakness and indecision demoralize the people and government of the victimized country, which encourages the mullahs to commit more terrorist acts to weaken them still further. By this means the cycle of terrorism grows and gathers more momentum.

The only way to end the cycle of terrorism is to take effective action against terrorism. President Bush has done this in Afghanistan and Iraq, and the Khomeini outlaw regime fears that Iran may be next. Rafsanjani has moved billions of dollars out of Iran, so that he can live in comfort if he has to flee the country. It is America's responsibility to exploit that fear by giving pro-democracy Iranians and Iranian-Americans the tools they need to topple the Khomeini outlaw regime and bring democracy back to Iran.

The constitutionalist democracy of 1906-1911 is ready for revival, and this time the United States will help protect it from foreign armies, something that was not possible 100 years ago. A free and democratic Iran would be a major victory in the war on terrorism, and the United States is committed to doing whatever it takes to win that war.

Chapter 10

The Iranian Government's Crimes Against America

Ayatollah Khomeini always hated America with a passion. His campaign of terrorism against America began when he took over the active management of the Iranian hostage crisis of 1979. This hatred is still being felt today, though Khomeini himself died in 1989, heart-broken that he had never conquered Iraq, Saudi Arabia, and the tiny oil-rich nations of the Persian Gulf. He dearly wanted to see Iranian tanks and aircraft entering Israel and Lebanon, but those tanks and aircraft needed American parts in order to run. And those parts became unavailable due to the hostage crisis.

Opinions differ on whether Khomeini was personally involved in planning the initial kidnapping of the United States Embassy personnel on November 4, 1979[139], but it is beyond dispute that within a short time, the kidnappers were taking orders from him. If he had ordered the hostages executed, they would have done it. Instead Khomeini used the hostages to test what degree of strength, courage, aggressiveness, and resolve the government of President Carter had.

Carter passed the test for resolve in that he never forgot, overlooked, or ignored the hostages, but he did not do well on the other tests. For example:

Low aggressiveness score: Carter never made a strong show of force to the Iranians. He never had our Navy anchor off the Iranian coast or taunt Khomeini's forces, the way President Reagan did with

Khomeini supporters with an American hostage

the Libyans. The only hostages he took were dollars, which didn't intimidate Khomeini at all. Carter was careful to make sure everyone knew his retaliatory measures were designed to prevent any loss of human life on either side. Among civilized people this might have earned Carter extra respect and prestige, but with the mullahs it earned him a low score for aggressiveness.

Low strength score: During the Carter years (1976-1980), America was still in shock at losing the Vietnam War. Many Americans had not then figured out that the enemy defeated us by dividing us politically, not by winning on the field of in battle. President Carter and his Congress responded to the feelings of the time by reducing the strength of the CIA and the American armed services to the point that they were short on equipment and experienced personnel. As a result, Carter's one attempt to rescue the hostages failed. Several of the rescue pilots were not familiar with the helicopters they were flying, and when a desert sandstorm came up, three of the helicopters stopped working. Another helicopter crashed into a refueling plane it could not see, and several lives were lost. The mission was aborted and the survivors returned to headquarters. The mullahs won without even firing a shot.

Low subversiveness score: The CIA did not mobilize Iranian opposition groups to subvert the Iranian government, the way they did in 1953. The CIA did not even have operatives in Iran at that time, notwithstanding the Iranian government's claims to the contrary. If President Carter had ordered the CIA to plan a coup, they would at least have tried. Khomeini was weaker then. Unfortunately, Carter would not seriously consider this. The inevitable comparisons with the overthrow of Mossadegh in 1953 would have been embarrassing, and his credentials as a liberal Democrat would have been damaged. In addition, Carter tended to focus on the personal aspects of the crisis, the well-being of the hostages, and to overlook the long -term geopolitical aspects of the replacement of the America-hating Khomeini regime with a more democratic and less hostile government in which every Iranian voice could be heard.

Low effectiveness score: Carter's responses to the hostage crisis consisted of talking, ordering a trade embargo, and freezing Iranian assets in the United States. He tried to hurt the mullahs in their pocketbooks. But the mullahs did not care. Money was not that important to the Khomeini outlaw regime in its early years. When they took over the Iranian embassy in the United States, they poured hundreds of thousands of dollars of liquor down the drain rather than sell it to non-Moslems for a profit. It was more important to them to show that they were different from the shah than to pick up some badly needed hard currency. Thus Carter's economic counterattack was seen as a minor irritant, not a devastating counterstrategy.

Low courage score: Carter avoided speaking or acting aggressively, for fear of endangering the hostages. This tactic was successful, inasmuch as none of them were maimed or killed, but it convinced the mullahs that he was a coward. Carter did serve in the American military in his younger days, but his service was aboard a submarine that never attacked or sank any other vessels. Thus his military background could not compensate for his meek and mild manner.

The greatest violence President Carter inflicted on anything during the hostage crisis was toward a rabbit. He was alone in a rowboat

Two helicopters that crashed during the unsuccessful attempt to rescue the hostages

on a lake, when a swimming rabbit approached and tried to board. He panicked and struck the rabbit violently with an oar until it gave up and swam away.

Carter told his aides about it when he got back to shore. Some of them told the press, and soon the story was known all over the world.

It is hard to imagine better news for Khomeini's terrorists than this story. The president of the United States was afraid of a rabbit! Their only regret was that Carter could not be president for life. They kept the hostages for the rest of Carter's term, then allowed their plane to take off one minute after President Reagan was sworn into office. The hostages were flown from Tehran to West Germany, where Carter met them personally (as President Reagan's special envoy) and Air Force doctors gave them thorough medical examinations.

The Iranian government gave President Carter another test, and he did poorly on that one as well. In July 1980, the Iranian government murdered an Iranian citizen in the United States. His name was Ali Akbar Tabatabai[140]. He was the head of the Iranian Freedom Foundation and a leading critic of Khomeini. He was killed by an American hired for the job. The killer disguised himself as a postman and shot Tabatabai at close range. The killer afterward flew to Switzerland, obtained a visa, and went to Iran. He married an Iranian woman, settled down, and has defeated all attempts to extradite him for the crime[141]. He claims to feel no remorse[142]. In 2001 he appeared in the film *Kandahar* under the name Hassan Tantai, allegedly without the director knowing about his murderous past[143].

The Khomeini government watched closely to see how the Carter administration would respond to this political killing in their own back yard. Would they demand extradition of the killer? Would they kill Khomeini supporters or burn down a building in revenge? What would they do?

The Carter administration, so far as is known, did nothing. This is not Carter's fault since the killing took place in Maryland and was therefore investigated by state and local agencies, not the federal government. But Khomeini's ignorance of America was enormous. He assumed that any killing of a political dissident would interest the federal government, and Carter's failure to respond was taken as further evidence that America was a weak and cowardly nation that had lost its way after losing the Vietnam War. For Khomeini that meant it was time to begin a campaign of crimes and terrorism against America, and that is what he did. The Khomeini outlaw regime is still at it, more than twenty-five years later.

In 1983 and 1984, during the Reagan administration, the Iranian government planned and executed major crimes against the United States, in which hundreds of Americans were killed. These crimes occurred in Beirut, Lebanon, and consisted of a series of bombings of the United States Embassy, the United States Consulate, and barracks of the United States Marine Corps.

After investigating, the Reagan administration decided there was no purpose to be served by keeping American troops in Lebanon. Nothing of value could be accomplished, and other nations that had troops there, such as Iran and Syria, were suffering thousands of casualties. President Reagan pulled our troops out to avoid the further loss of American lives. Unfortunately, it once again appeared that Americans were cowardly, and the terrorists drew encouragement from this.

The bombings were carried out by members of Hezbollah, the Lebanese terrorist organization created by the Iranian government. They also kidnapped and killed Robert Stethem, a United States Navy diver, and a CIA Station Chief, Col. William F. Buckley. By using Hezbollah, the Iranian government hid its tracks from those unaware of the relationship.

More than 240 U. S. Marines were killed in Lebanon, and none of the killers were punished for their deeds. President Reagan had the U.S.S. *New Jersey* shell a number of enemy positions, but other than that, there was no reprisal.

The terrorists had no navy, and the Iranian navy had no ships in the Mediterranean Sea, so they were unable to respond to the shelling. The U.S.S. *New Jersey* finished its business, sailed away, and they were powerless to stop it.

The Iranian government stepped up the pace against America in the 1990s, with still more bombings, such as the Khobar Towers in Saudi Arabia (1996) and the U. S. Embassies in Kenya and Tanzania (1998). The Khobar Towers bombing was initially attributed to Hezbollah, while al Qaeda was blamed for the embassy attacks. But again, the crimes were planned, organized, and financed by the Iranian government.

They also sabotaged President Clinton's attempts to negotiate a lasting peace between the Israelis and the Palestinians. Whenever a major success appeared likely, the Iranian government would direct a series of terrorist attacks, usually suicide bombers, to kill Israelis. The Israeli government would then retaliate with attacks that killed Palestinians, which would outrage the Palestinians and kill any potential settlement.

So far the War on Terror has not discouraged the Iranian government from planning and financing terrorist attacks against Americans. They financed five simultaneous bombing attacks in Casablanca, Morocco, and three simultaneous bombings in Riyadh, Saudi Arabia. Al Qaeda was happy to take all the credit, because America was already at war with them and they wanted a boost in prestige in the Islamic world.

In 2004 the Iranian government backed repeated attacks on American soldiers and civilians of all nations. They have operated through at least three different fronts: Hojatolislam Muqtada al Sadr, terrorist Abu Musab al Zarkawi, and the Iranian Revolutionary Guard.

The Iranian government has also attempted to outflank the American forces by placing Shahab missiles on both sides of Iraq, in Iran to the east and Syria and Lebanon to the west. The missiles in Syria and Lebanon were given to Hezbollah. This was probably intended to reduce the Iranian government's risk of war with the United States. Iran has a mutual defense treaty with the governments of Syria and Lebanon and theoretically must come to their defense if they get into an armed conflict with the United States. Hezbollah is not a nation so by blaming any attacks on them, Lebanon and Syria can claim they were not responsible.

This approach relies on the assumption that Hezbollah can always be controlled by Iran and will not fall into the hands of a renegade leader who does not care about Iranian money. So far this assumption has proven accurate.

This tactic may not work with America. President Bush has already announced that in his eyes, any country harboring or helping terrorists is just as much an enemy as the terrorists themselves. If the governments of Syria and Lebanon fail to control Hezbollah's missiles, they can expect to be treated the same way as if they launched the missiles themselves. The president of Lebanon has already anticipated this possibility. He dealt with it by resigning from office.

A complete list of the Iranian government's crimes against America and Americans would be a long one. It seems likely that at least some of the terrorist attacks launched in other parts of the world, such as Bali, the Philippines, and Pakistan, were financed by Iran but carried out by local terrorists. It is a win-win proposition for both sets of killers. It is the peace-loving majority of people world-wide who lose. We can greatly reduce the flow of losses by putting the Iranian government out of business and letting the decent people of Iran control their country's destiny. And the world will rejoice when these criminals are finally brought to justice.

Chapter 11

Iran's Nuclear Weapons Program

Knowing what we know about the flagrantly wicked nature of the Iranian government, imagine how much worse they would be if they had nuclear weapons! Unfortunately, this is not just imagination. If nothing interferes with its plans, the Iranian government will have nuclear weapons by 2005 or 2006. These will not be North Korean imports but rather domestically produced atomic bombs. Iran's bomb factories will be able to make more of them as long as Iran's supplies of uranium and plutonium hold up. The uranium and plutonium will come from Iran's nuclear reactors, and the mullahs plan to build a lot of them.

The Khomeini outlaw regime has been working on atomic bombs for over ten years, with the help of technicians from North Korea, Russia, and other countries. This is officially denied, but almost nobody is fooled by the denials.

A quick look at the history of nuclear weapons is all we need to see why nobody in the Khomeini outlaw regime should be allowed to have them.

The first nuclear weapons were used in World War II. Months after Germany and Italy had surrendered, Japan continued fighting. Two atomic bombs were dropped on Japanese cities in August of 1945, and the Japanese government surrendered on September 2, 1945.

General George C. Marshall, the U. S. Army chief of staff at the time, said that the United States did not expect the Japanese government to surrender as a result of the bombs. They thought a massive invasion of Japan would be necessary to end the war. The invasion plans included the dropping of twelve atomic bombs to soften resistance and make it easier for the American troops to land[144]. Fortunately for everyone, these plans never had to be carried out.

Atomic bombs, now known as nuclear weapons, were so terrifying that nobody criticized the Japanese decision to surrender. It was generally believed that the use of such weapons could mean the end of civilization, or even the end of life on earth.

The fear of nuclear weapons and nuclear warfare remained strong during the 1950s and did not die down until the late 1960s. Fortunately, the countries that had nuclear weapons at that time worked hard to avoid having to use them. None of the first five nuclear powers—Britain, China, France, the Soviet Union, and the United States—has fought a major battle with any of the others for more than fifty years.

The Vietnam War took America's attention away from nuclear warfare and eventually proved that having nuclear weapons does not guarantee victory. North Vietnam, a small nation with no nuclear weapons, conquered South Vietnam despite American military opposition. The Americans never lost a major battle, but the North Vietnamese won the war, through a superior propaganda campaign that deeply divided the American people. The aftereffects were felt as recently as the presidential campaign of 2004, in which one of the candidates spoke more about his four months of combat experience in Vietnam[145] than his nineteen years in the U. S. Senate.

The Soviet war in Afghanistan in the 1980s had a similar outcome. The Soviets outnumbered the Afghanis about 15 to 1, but ultimately they gave up and went home. Once again, a small non-nuclear country prevailed against a nuclear superpower. Neither superpower ever made serious threats to use its nuclear weapons against the smaller country.

Similarly, Great Britain never threatened to use them in the Falklands War with Argentina, France never threatened to use them in its police actions in Africa, and China never threatened to use them in its wars with Vietnam and India.

Nuclear weapons have not lost their power to kill and destroy. Their destructive power is measured in terms of how many millions of tons of dynamite it would take to do the same amount of damage. A fifty megaton bomb does as much damage as 100 billion pounds (50,000,000 tons) of dynamite.

But does Iran have nuclear weapons yet? Nobody outside Iran knows for sure. The best guess is that Iran will have them by 2005 or 2006 at the latest. Once they do, it will be impossible to turn back the clock. Very few governments have given up nuclear weapons once they had them[146]. There is no reason to expect Iran to be different.

The Iranian government has invested heavily in weapons. In 1996 Iran signed an agreement to buy 4.5 billion dollars in arms from China. The purchase included military aircraft, armored vehicles, naval vessels, missiles and missile launchers. They have also purchased anti-ship cruise missiles and fast naval attack vessels[147].

The Iranian government also wants all three kinds of weapons of mass destruction: chemical, biological, and nuclear. One of America's most successful generals of the early twenty-first century, General Mike DeLong (USMC) has already warned us about this.

> We know that Iran and Syria were making chemical and biological weapons at an unprecedented rate before the Iraq War and continue to do so today. We know that Syria was a hiding place for Iraqi WMD [weapons of mass destruction]. We know that Syria provided safe haven for Saddam sympathizers and both Syria and Iran are harboring al-Qaeda and other terrorist organizations. And we know they are sponsoring terrorists and sending suicide bombers across their borders into Iraq. Most troubling of all is Iran's rapid pursuit of developing nuclear weapons. Syria and Iran are problem countries that have to be dealt with[148].

Nuclear weapons are by far the deadliest of the three types of weapons of mass destruction. A nuclear explosion can kill more than 250,000 people in under an hour and leave radioactive waste that will last for 10,000 years. Chemical and biological weapons kill far fewer people and are harder to control. Chemical weapons in particular tend to dissipate and break down after they come into contact with the air. Most observers would agree that Iran's nuclear weapons program is a greater threat than its stockpiles of chemical and biological weapons.

Both Khatami and Khamenei have stated that Iran is not developing nuclear weapons, because they are somehow "unIslamic". These are lies, of course. Regardless of who wins the 2005 Iranian presidential campaign, we can expect increased spending on nuclear weapons development as long as the price of oil stays high.

During the 1990s the Iranian government acquired "dual use technology" — equipment that can be used either to make nuclear weapons or to generate nuclear energy. Examples would include Iran's nuclear reactors, nuclear power plants, gas centrifuge technology, a uranium conversion plant, and a laser isotope separator that can be used for enrichment[149]. Iran does not really need nuclear power, because their natural gas deposits can generate more than enough energy for its needs.

During the 1990s the United States was aware of Iran's proliferation of weapons of mass destruction. A state of emergency was declared in 1994, and a few years later, Congress passed the Iran Missile Proliferation Sanctions Act of 1998, which required the president to impose sanctions on Russian companies that helped Iran's missile program.

President Clinton vetoed the Iran Missile Proliferation Sanctions Act of 1998 but then issued executive orders imposing sanctions on ten Russian companies between June 1998 and January 1999. They had no impact on either the companies or Iran.

Two years later, Congress passed the Iran Nonproliferation Act of 2000, which requires the president to regularly give Congress lists of entities that are helping Iranian weapons of mass destruction programs. The president is granted the power to prohibit the export of arms or dual-use equipment to those entities[150].

President Bush has consistently maintained that the Iranian government is attempting to develop and manufacture nuclear weapons. His press secretary summarized this position in a press conference with former U.S. press secretary, Ari Fleischer:

Q How concerned is the President over Iran's apparent progress with their nuclear program, and what is the United States response going to be to that?

MR. FLEISCHER: We have long made clear our concerns about Iran's pursuit of nuclear weapons, as well as other weapons of mass destruction. Iran now openly says that it is pursuing a complete nuclear fuel cycle. We completely reject Iran's claim that it is doing so for peaceful purposes. After all, Iran has been in possession of a great amount of energy of a non-nuclear nature as a result of their gas and oil supplies.

Iran attempted to construct in secret a uranium enrichment plant and heavy water plant. The first could be used to produce highly enriched uranium for weapons; the second could support a reactor for producing weapons-grade plutonium. Iran admitted the existence of these facilities only after it had no choice, only because they had been made public by an Iranian opposition group.

And it is also worth noting that . . . Iran was far, far ahead of where they were believed to be in the development of this. And if it had not been for the Iranian opposition group, this, too, may have gone unnoticed . . . [151]

The Iranian government has tried to reduce President Bush's influence by cultivating Senator Joe Biden (D-MD), the senior Democrat on the Senate Foreign Relations Committee. In February 2002, one of their American lobbyists, Dr. Sadegh Namazi-khan, held a fundraiser for Senator Biden at his home, in the name of the Iranian Muslim Association of North America[152]. The fundraiser brought in roughly $30,000 for Senator Biden's reelection campaign[153].

The following year Senator Biden urged the White House to take a go-slow approach to Iran and finish its missions in Iraq and Afghanistan first[154]. However, he also said, "We know that they are developing a nuclear weapons program. They've been doing that for the last ten years, although the International Atomic Energy Agency is in there."[155].

In January 2004, Senator Biden met with Iranian Foreign Minister Kamal Kharrazi at an economic conference in Davos, Switzerland[156]. Senator Biden said some friendly words and condemned President

Inside the Bushehr nuclear reactor.

Bush's Iran policy, but he did not endorse Iran's nuclear weapons program or say that it was not a problem.

Thus the political efforts of the Iranian government in America have yielded few useful results. Senator Biden has not taken high profile positions in favor of the Khomeini outlaw regime, and his criticisms of President Bush have been less extreme than those of other Democrats, such as former United States Senator Tom Daschle.

Americans in both major political parties consider the nuclear weapons program to be a serious menace, and they refuse to believe that the Iranian government wants uranium, plutonium, and long range missiles only for peaceful purposes. This universal disbelief is based on clear and objective facts.

One of the elements in the nuclear weapons program is the Bushehr nuclear power plant. Construction was begun by German companies in 1975 and resumed by the Russians after the end of the Iraq-Iran War. Its normal operations will produce the type of uranium needed for making nuclear weapons, such as atomic bombs and missiles with nuclear warheads.

In 1995 Russia and Iran entered into a new agreement under which the Russians agreed to do further work on Bushehr. They also agreed to sell four million pounds (2,000 tons) of uranium and help develop a uranium mine in Iran, low-power training reactors, a gas centrifuge plant, an option on a light-water research reactor, a nuclear-powered desalinization plant, and training for ten to twenty high level nuclear employees each year. The Clinton Administration confronted the Russian government about these commitments during a summit conference.

The Russians agreed to cancel everything except the Bushehr power plant, and in December 1995 the agreement was finalized between Vice President Gore and Prime Minister Chernomyrdin. Five years later, in December 2000, the Russians renounced the Gore-Chernomyrdin agreement and stated that they no longer considered it binding. The Russians made this announcement while Vice President Gore was busily involved in lawsuits concerning the 2000 presidential election, in the hope that neither Gore nor the Western media would pay much attention to it.

Since the repudiation of the Gore-Chernomyrdin agreement,

A major uranium-enrichment plant has been discovered in Natanz[157];

A test run of gas centrifuges has been done in Kalaye;

One thousand kilograms [2,200 pounds/1.1 tons] of uranium hexafluoride have been discovered in storage in Tehran;

A new nuclear test facility has been discovered—the Jabr

Ibn Hayan Multipurpose Laboratories in Tehran;

Iran has admitted buying 400 kilograms [880 pounds] of uranium tetrafluoride from the Chinese and converting it to metallic uranium, which is useless for light-water nuclear reactors but can be used to make atomic bombs[158];

A heavy-water production plant is under construction at Arak[159];

A nuclear fuel plant will be built at Isfahan[160];

Two new uranium enrichment plants, in the villages of Lashkar-Abad and Ramandeh, both about twenty-four miles west of Tehran (and close to each other);

In 2001, Iran's President Khatami signed an arms deal with the Russians worth $7 billion[161];

In June of 2003, three inspectors from the IAEA were physically prevented from taking soil samples to test for the presence of nuclear material[162].

Clearly the notion that Iran is interested only in building nuclear energy plants does not stand up when examined. One of the flaws in this argument was explained succinctly in a speech by U.S. Assistant Secretary of State John Wolf:

> "There can be no logical explanation for a country like Iran, so rich in oil and natural gas, to spend billions of dollars to establish an entire nuclear fuel cycle. The gas they flare annually is worth considerably more than the price they are paying for Bushehr, and that's but one of the nuclear efforts under way. We're confident of our intelligence, which shows conclusively that Iran's objective is early acquisition of a nuclear weapons capability[163].

In short, they are not building nuclear reactors for energy, but rather to refine uranium for atomic bombs. Their nuclear weapons program seeks to acquire more power and more legitimacy in the eyes of their friends and supporters.

If they succeed, it will usher in a whole new era of terrorism. It is one thing for terrorists to shoot four people in the Mykonos Restaurant and quite another to set off an atomic bomb there that destroys half of Berlin.

Rafsanjani has already expressed the opinion that the Islamic World could win a nuclear war with Israel, saying, "Application of an atomic bomb would not leave anything in Israel but the same thing would just produce damages in the Muslim world."[164]

After Rafsanjani made these remarks, people in Iran and elsewhere debated why he had made them. The one thing that nobody questioned was his sincerity: he not only thinks that a nuclear war between Iran and Israel is winnable, he also seems to think it is a good idea. All that stops him from testing this theory is the lack of nuclear weapons. The Iranian government is trying to build them as quickly as it can, and the best guess is that they will have them before the end of 2006. Outside efforts to slow down their program can achieve little at this point.

The Iranian government was aware of that when it agreed with Britain, France, and Germany to temporarily stop enriching uranium. All the agreement did was reduce tension and buy a little time. No real reforms were achieved.

The Iranian government can resume uranium enrichment at any time, and it can continue designing atomic bombs and nuclear missiles. Iran does not need more weapons-grade uranium until the bomb casings and missile housings have been built, and it still has tons of less refined uranium acquired over the years. Once the bombs and missiles are ready for loading, Iran can resume the enrichment program where it left off[165].

If the Khomeini outlaw regime is still in power when the nuclear weapons are ready, what will they do with them?

Their history of terrorism by proxy suggests that the Khomeini outlaw regime might give some of their smaller nukes to Hezbollah and al Qaeda to use against the United States, Israel, Saudi Arabia, and possibly Iraq. Those outfits could keep them, use them, or sell them to other terrorist organizations, such as:

The Chechen terrorists for use against Russia,

The Uighur separatist terrorists for use against China,

The Islamic terrorists of Thailand for use in Southeast Asia,

The Kashmiri terrorists for use against India,

The Irish Republican Army, for use against the British, or

Any of the European terrorist groups for use on that continent.

However, al Qaeda would be more likely to keep their nuclear weapons or use them against the United States, rather than selling them to raise money. Al Qaeda is usually able to raise funds through extortion, racketeering, and voluntary donations. Al Qaeda has set official goals of:

killing two million American children,

killing two million American adults,

rendering eight million Americans homeless, and

crippling hundreds of thousands of additional Americans[166].

They claim that this is what America has done to Arabs, both directly and by supporting Israel. By this logic, they are only trying to achieve "parity".

Nuclear weapons would help al Qaeda achieve this destruction quota more quickly, with less time and effort[167]. As far back as December 1998, Osama bin Laden told Time Magazine that acquiring nuclear weapons "in defense of Muslims" was a religious duty[168]. And there are signs that he has tried to acquire nuclear weapons capability.

> On September 25, 1998, German police arrested Mamdouh Mahmud Salim and charged him with trying to obtain highly enriched uranium.

> In late 1998 Arabic media claimed that bin Laden was hiring nuclear scientists, trying to buy "suitcase" nuclear bombs, and trying to create his own manufacturing plant for nuclear weapons.

> Two top Pakistani nuclear scientists, Sultan Bashiruddin Mahmood and Abdul Majid, discussed nuclear, chemical, and biological weapons with Osama bin Laden. Mahmood thinks that all Islamic countries should have nuclear weapons[169].

If the Iranian government ever gives bin Laden the chance to buy nuclear weapons, he will buy them. This is a man who once paid $30,000,000 to Chechnyan kidnappers to murder four British men, after they had agreed to accept a $10,000,000 ransom from their employer[170].

Hezbollah would also like to get nuclear weapons from Iran. The Iranian government recently gave them over 200 short-range missiles[171], and they would love to put nuclear warheads in them. Their closest target would most likely be Israel, but that would not be their only target.

Hezbollah has not attacked Americans on American soil, but in 2003, Hezbollah's Secretary-General, Sheikh Hassan Nasrallah, said, "Death to America is, and will stay our slogan."[172] In Iraq, Hezbollah agents have been monitoring and photographing American soldiers and sending the results to the Iranian Revolutionary Guards[173]. Hezbollah considers Khomeini its chief spiritual mentor and inspiration[174], and the Khomeini outlaw regime is its chief banker. On October 31, 2004, members of the Iranian Majlis also cried "Death to America" as they voted unanimously in favor of a resolution requiring the government to continue its uranium enrichment activities[175]. The bill requires the Iranian government to make every effort to gain access to nuclear technology, including the complete nuclear fuel cycle necessary to make uranium pure enough for nuclear weapons[176].

The Iranian government has been planning the destruction of the United States for years, and nuclear weapons would greatly strengthen their hand. Fear is how the Khomeini outlaw regime expands its influence in the world, and few things are more frightening than nuclear weapons. Many of the Khomeini outlaw regime insiders agree with the retired Arab general who once told al Jazeera, "We are no less than the Vietnamese. Just make it costly in body bags and the Americans will run."[177]

The Iranian government's plans to destroy America were made crystal clear by Dr. Hassan Abbassi, the chairman of the Iranian Revolutionary Guards' Center for Doctrinaire Affairs of National Security Outside Iran's Borders. Here are a few of his remarks.

"We have a strategy drawn up for the destruction of Anglo-Saxon civilization and for the uprooting of the Americans and the English. Our missiles are now ready to strike at their civilization, and as soon as the instructions arrive from Leader [Ali Khamenei], we will launch our missiles at their cities and installations. Our motto during the war in Iraq was: Karbala, we are coming, Jerusalem, we are coming. The global infidel front is a front against Allah and the Muslims, and we must make use of everything we have at hand to strike at this front, by means of our suicide operations or by means of our missiles[178].

"Our intention is that 6,000 United States nuclear warheads will explode in [the United States]. We have located the weak points and we have transferred the information about them to the guerilla organizations, and we are acting through them . . .

"We have established a department for Britain as well, and the discussion about bringing about its collapse is on our agenda. We are also operating among the Mexicans, the Argentineans, and all those with a problem with the United States."[179]

More recently an Iranian newspaper publisher named Shariatmadari (not the deceased ayatollah) recruited 25,000 Iranians to attack targets inside the United States. His recruiting technique included nonstop references to the Abu Ghraib prison scandal and the outrageous lie that American soldiers have raped 20,000 Iraqi women. He argued that if American soldiers came to Iran, they would treat Iranian women the same way. Many of the Khomeini outlaw regime mullahs have been saying the same things in their mosques throughout the country. Unfortunately, many of the recruits believe these stories.

Mr. Shariatmadari is not the only one calling for genocide against Americans. On the twenty-first anniversary of the bombing of the U.S. Marine Corps barracks in Beirut, a ceremony for 200 newly recruited suicide bombers was held in a cemetery in Tehran. It was organized by a private Islamic fascist organization, the Headquarters for Commemorating Martyrs of the Global Islamic Movement. A spokesman called the new recruits the "first suicide commando unit,"[180], apparently forgetting the nine-year old- boys who died running through mine fields during the Iran-Iraq War.

The group's commitment to genocide applies not just to Americans, but to all blasphemous occupiers of Islamic lands[181]. They also unveiled a two meter stone column commemorating the murder of the U.S. Marines.

Imagine what could happen if each of these 200 bombers was given a suitcase-sized nuclear weapon and dropped off near the Canadian or Mexican border, with instructions to enter the United States and blow up a major city. If ninety-seven percent of them were detected and captured by the authorities, a phenomenal success ratio,

Shariat-Madari's newspaper article "We Shall Never Allow Americans and Europeans to Have Security in Their Own Cities". The article calls for 25,000 Iranians to become suicide bombers.

the other three percent would still bring nuclear destruction to six American cities.

Right now Iran is busy refining and enriching the uranium needed for these bombs. Our window of opportunity to prevent this is still open, but not for much longer.

The Iranian government secretly supports the Headquarters for Commemorating Martyrs of the Global Islamic Movement while officially claiming not to and asserting that it will be allowed to operate only as long as its ideas are limited to theory and not action[182]. It seems likely that Khamenei and Rafsanjani are the ones to decide if and when this group crosses the line from theory to action and which of its leaders will be used as scapegoats if their attacks backfire. In the meantime, the Iranian government is attempting to intimidate the United States by boasting about its missile capabilities.

General Yadollah Javani, the head of the Political Bureau of the Iranian Revolutionary Guards, wrote in an editorial that Iran has "long-range smart missiles which can reach many of the interests and vital resources of the Americans and of the Zionist regime in our region"[183]. It is unclear whether he was referring to the Shahab-4 and Shahab-5 missile program, which recently received one billion dollars in funding from Khamenei. Supposedly the Shahab-3 missiles are

125

ready for mass production. They normally have a range of 800 to 1000 miles, but Defense Minister Ali Shamkhani claims that they have been upgraded to a range of 1,250 miles[184].

The money for these missile programs came from increased oil revenues, resulting from the higher oil prices in 2004. The price of oil is expected to remain high for some time, because of the increase in demand in China, India, and other Asian countries and the shortage of refineries to process crude oil into gasoline and other petroleum products. High oil prices will only make it easier for Khamenei to continue spending billions of dollars to develop long range missiles.

Iranian politicians have already threatened to make preemptive missile strikes against American forces in the Middle East, if necessary to prevent attacks on Iran's nuclear facilities. Iran's defense minister, Rear Admiral Shamkhani, made the threat during an al Jazeera interview on August 18, 2004. Shamkhani is a former presidential candidate and could run again if Rafsanjani does not.

> "We will not sit with arms folded to wait for what others will do to us. Some military commanders in Iran are convinced that preventive operations which the Americans talk about are not their monopoly. America is not the only one present in the region. We are also present, from Khost to Kandahar in Afghanistan; *we are present in the Gulf and we can be present in Iraq.* [emphasis added]

> "The United States military presence in Iraq will not become an element of strength at our expense. The opposite is true, because their forces would turn into a hostage in the event of an attack.[185]

Iran has entered into a mutual defense treaty with Syria and Lebanon, which provides that Iran will help defend those countries if attacked by either Israel or the United States. The treaty was negotiated by Rear Admiral Shamkhani in March of 2004 and has been praised by both Syrian and Lebanese leaders. The treaty makes it politically easy for Iran to move troops, tanks, and missiles into Syria and Lebanon. Logistically they would have to pass through northern Iraq or southeastern Turkey in order to get from Iran to Syria. Turkey is unlikely to allow Iranian troops on its soil, but if Iraq fell apart into a

Female volunteers for the first crop of Iranian suicide bombers. They were recruited by the Headquarters for Commemorating Martyrs of the Global Islamic Movement, a private Islamic fascist organization.

collection of tiny states, Iran might well be able to bribe, bully, or subvert the inhabitants of the northern region to allow Iranian troops to pass.

This could set the stage for a terrorist attack on Israel, with Iranian troops attacking from the north and northeast, and Saudi Wahabbis attacking from the south and southeast. The Iranian missiles in Lebanon could theoretically be used to keep the U. S. Seventh Fleet at least 200 miles away from the Israeli coastline during such an attack, though there are doubts as to how effective such intimidation would be.

By establishing this new military alliance, the terrorist government of Iran has laid the groundwork for further destabilizing the situation in the Middle East. If it manages, by threats and terrorist attacks, to drive the Americans out of the area, the danger of destabilization, collapse, and all-out warfare will increase dramatically.

The United States cannot and will not be intimidated by Iranian government threats. Our troops are next door in Iraq, and they are better trained and equipped than Iran's. The Iranians were unable to defeat Saddam Hussein after eight years of warfare and more than one million deaths. The United States defeated him in less than a month, with fewer than 1,000 deaths.

Despite this, or perhaps because of it, the Iranian government hates us, fears us, and wants to destroy us. We cannot allow it to do that. The situation we face today is similar to the situation Britain and France faced in 1936 when Adolf Hitler became the chancellor of Germany. His army was weaker then, and if they had attacked him in 1936, many lives could have been saved on both sides. There would have been no V-2 rocket attacks on London, no German occupation of Paris, and the fire-bombing of Dresden might not have been necessary.

Instead, Britain and France negotiated with Hitler, gave him what he wanted, and let him grow stronger and stronger. They let Hitler decide when and where to start the war. He chose Poland on September 1, 1939. Hitler was a clever man, much like Rafsanjani, Mugniyeh, and Nateq-Nouri. Hitler chose so well that the United States stayed out of the fight for two years, and the Soviet Union stayed out until Germany attacked it. The Allies eventually won, but the war claimed over fifty million lives.

We do not want to make a similar mistake with the Khomeini outlaw regime. Hitler never had nuclear weapons, but Iran will have them in two years or less. It is essential for Iran to become a democracy before that happens, so that her nuclear arsenal is controlled by people who value freedom and democracy far more than political dominance.

Chapter 12

Iran's Missile Program

The leaders of North Korea hate the United States as much as Khomeini did. Over fifty years ago we prevented the North Koreans from conquering South Korea, and they still hate us for it. This hatred, combined with a need for hard currency, gives them an understandable inclination to sell missiles and missile technology to the Iranian government.

Iran has bought missiles from other countries as well, but when Iran started its own missile program, the mullahs decided to model their missiles after North Korea's missiles.

The Shahab-1 and Shahab-2 missiles are modeled after North Korean Scud missiles. They have ranges of roughly 200 miles (320km) and 310 miles (500 km) respectively. One Western source estimates the Iranian government had about 400 of these (combined) as of 2001[186]. The number is probably larger today. Iran recently gave over 200 of them to Hezbollah to deploy in Lebanon.

The Shahab-3 missile is modeled after North Korea's Nodong-1 missile and has a range of about 800 miles (1300 km). This missile was tested several times over a five-year period[187] and pronounced ready for production in June of 2003. The Shahab-3 missile could reach Israel from Syria, Lebanon, or western Iran, and it could carry a nuclear warhead.

The Shahab-4 and Shahab-5 missiles are even scarier. The Shahab-4 is designed to fly 2800 kilometers [1740 miles], while the

Shahab-5 is designed for a range of 4900 kilometers [3045 miles] to 5300 kilometers [3290 miles]. They are not yet ready for production, but after Israel's threat in 2004 to prevent Iran from building any nuclear weapons, Khamenei gave one billion dollars to the Ministry of Defense to resume work on them[188].

In November of 2004 Defense Minister Ali Shamkhani asserted that Iran was not producing on any missiles with a range greater than the 1,250 mile radius of the upgraded Shahab-3 missiles[189]. It seems likely that he meant the Shahab-4 and Shahab-5 are still in the development phase and are not yet reliable enough for production.

In a sermon on December 14, 2001, while the Shahab-3 was still in the testing phase, Ayatollah Rafsanjani said that if the Islamic world had nuclear weapons, ". . . application of an atomic bomb would not leave anything in Israel, but the same thing would just produce damages in the Muslim world."[190]. The words are chilling, and he has never retracted them.

General John Abizaid of the United States Army has told Congress, "Iran has the largest ballistic missile inventory in the Central Command region to include long-range weapons of mass destruction and delivery systems capable of reaching deployed United States forces in the theater . . . Iran casts a shadow on security and stability in the Gulf region. Iran's military is second only to the United States. United States allies in the Gulf acknowledge Iran's increasingly proactive efforts to soften its image and appear less hegemonic; however, Iran's military poses a potential threat to neighboring countries."[191]

The United States has tried to discourage foreign companies from helping the Iranian missile program by levying economic sanctions. They have had little effect because most of the companies selling to Iran are not doing business with the United States. The United States has had somewhat better luck persuading foreign governments to place their own limits on the types of equipment and software that can be sold to Iran.

North Korea is immune to American threats of economic sanctions because they have been under a complete trade embargo for over fifty years. Its main concern has been delivering missiles to Iran without having them intercepted.

Shahab-3 missile with anti-American writing, roughly "We will trample America under our feet."

Until recent years the favorite way was by ship, but that has become riskier. In December 2002, a North Korean ship carrying missiles was stopped and searched by the United States Navy on the open seas. The ship was released after it was proven that the missiles had been bought by the government of Yemen for use against Yemenese rebels.

The North Koreans knew that if the missiles had been headed to Iran they would have been seized. Since that incident, no Western observers have seen any ships headed for Iran with North Korean missiles. Instead, the North Koreans have been disassembling the missiles into smaller parts and flying them to Iran.

Between April and June of 2003, Iranian IL-76 transport planes made six flights from Pyongyang, North Korea to Iran. South Korean and United States intelligence agencies concluded they were probably shipping disassembled warheads and missiles[192].

There are some indications that North Korea has supplied engineers to help the Iranian missile program. This makes sense, because North Korea already has missiles that can reach the United States.

> Unlike five years ago, North Korea can now [1999] strike the United States with a missile that could deliver high explosive, chemical, biological, or possibly nuclear weapons. Currently, the United States is unable to defend against this threat[193].

Once Iran has such missiles, it can threaten an enormous number of people, in Europe, the Middle East, and most of Africa.

As long as the mullahs are in power and oil prices are high, Iran will continue its missile program. It is vital for the Iranian people to replace the current government with a fair and democratic government that will never use such missiles except in defense.

It is probably not feasible to take nuclear weapons away from the Khomeini outlaw regime. Ironically, it is more practical to take the country away instead[194]. The Iranian people would have voted the mullahs out years ago if Iran had free and lawful elections. The Iranian people have no desire to see their country become like North Korea, and they have no desire to use nuclear weapons against anybody. They just want to lead normal productive lives free of government interference, like their Iranian-American relatives.

They have the desire for freedom and democracy; they simply need some tools, advice, and logistical support. The United States would gain a valuable ally, North Korea would lose one of its best customers, and every nation that has feared the Khomeini outlaw regime would breathe a sigh of relief.

Chapter 13

American Policy Toward Iran

The United States has had economic relations but little political involvement with Iran for most of America's history[195]. The first significant contacts occurred in the nineteenth century, when American merchant ships entered the Persian Gulf to do business. Trade built up to the point that in 1856 the United States and Persia entered into a trade treaty giving most favored nation status to each other. In 1883 the United States opened a permanent diplomatic mission in Tehran which lasted, in one form or another, until the Iranian Hostage crisis in 1979.

The Persians liked the Americans and tried to form alliances with them to get better leverage in dealing with the British and Russians. However, America was far away and had a tradition of avoiding alliances that could get us involved in European wars or politics.

America was also unwilling to interfere with the British, who were traditional friends. For these reasons and others, no military or political alliances were entered into between America and Persia in the nineteenth century or the first half of the twentieth century.

During World War II America sent 30,000 troops to Iran (the name changed from Persia to Iran in 1935). Their job was to transport trucks, weapons, supplies, and food to the Soviet army under the Lend Lease program.

Communications were not good because few Persian civilians along the transport route spoke English, and few American soldiers spoke Farsi. There were traffic accidents and some drunk driving problems, but in general the Americans behaved better than the thousands of British and Russian troops already in the country. The Iranians asked the Americans to kick the British and Russian troops out and make Lend Lease a one hundred percent American operation, but the request was politely turned down.

America did not want to antagonize its allies and did not want to remove troops from the war in the Pacific to transport supplies through Iran. However, President Roosevelt did persuade the British and Russian leaders to acknowledge in writing that the war effort was placing a burden on Iran, that Iranian independence should be recognized, and that all three countries would have their troops out of Iran within six months after the war ended.

America and Britain met the deadline, but the Russians ignored it. They sent 15,000 more troops into Iran, raising their total to 95,000. They also encouraged secession and rebellion among the Kurdish and Azeri populations in northwest Iran.

President Roosevelt was dead by then, but his successor, President Truman, was furious at this breach of Stalin's prior commitment. He ordered three American combat divisions in Austria to be ready to go to Iran. This got Stalin's attention, and in March 1946 the Russians announced that they would pull all their troops out of Iran[196]. They had all their troops out within sixty days, although at least 5,000 subversive agents remained in the country[197].

Persian diplomatic negotiations also played a part in this troop withdrawal, but the possibility of American military intervention was a major incentive for Stalin. As Al Capone once said, "You can get more with a smile and a gun than you can with just a smile."

President Truman's success had a tremendous impact on Iranians. They had been trying to get rid of the Russians for centuries, and the Americans accomplished it in less than a year, without a shot being fired. Understandably, this success caused many Iranians to see Americans as much stronger, more clever, and more influential than they really were.

This led the shah, among others, to seek closer military and economic relations with the United States. This fit in well with the Cold

War containment policy the Americans were adopting toward the Soviet Union, and in May of 1950 a mutual defense agreement was signed[198].

The Iranians did not know the Americans very well in those days. Many of them tended to view America's successes as evidence that America would control their country and destiny as the British and Russians had done before. At that time it was inconceivable for many Iranians that America had no interest in doing so, or that America did not want to steal their oil and minerals. They were simply not familiar with Westerners who did not act like European colonialists. Today the situation is different, due in part to the number of Iranian-Americans and their communications with family and friends in Iran.

The United States is one of the few countries ever to turn down an opportunity to obtain Iranian oil rights at a discount. In 1946 the shah offered oil rights to the United States in return for restoring his power, which was then very weak. The United States declined the offer. It was inconceivable to Americans that we would undermine the British oil interests in Iran, since Britain was an old friend and heavily dependent on Iranian oil.

Most Iranians would have preferred doing business with American oil companies, which were then offering 50-50 deals to other countries. The Anglo-Iranian Oil Company, by contrast, was paying a royalty of less than fifteen percent at that time and treating its Iranian employees very badly. The people running the company had difficulty understanding that the era of colonialism was over.

In 1949 the Iranians demanded a renegotiation of the British oil rights, hoping for a 50-50 deal such as the one that American oil companies negotiated with Venezuela. The Anglo-Iranian Oil Company was unwilling to do that, although it did submit offers that the Majlis then voted down. In November 1950 a consortium of American oil companies negotiated a new 50-50 deal with Saudi Arabia. The British ambassador to Iran recommended a similar deal for the Anglo-Iranian Oil Company. The British government and the Anglo-Iranian Oil Company immediately rejected his suggestion.

This infuriated the Iranians, and it increased the power of Muhammad Mossadegh, a member of the Majlis who had already advocated nationalizing the oil industry. In early 1951, a Majlis commission recommended full nationalization. Prime Minister Razmara rejected the recommendation and was assassinated less than a month later. The shah appointed Mossadegh to replace him, and on April 30, 1951, the full Majlis voted for nationalization. The shah signed the bill within forty-eight hours.

The British reaction was extreme. The Anglo-Iranian Oil Company shut down the oil fields, fired 20,000 employees, and organized an oil boycott. The British government began planning for an armed invasion of Iran with 70,000 soldiers[199]. Both the British and the Iranians called on the United States to take their side.

The American government was appalled at the thought of a British invasion because it would give the Soviet Union an excuse to invade from the north. It was hard for the Americans to feel much sympathy for the Anglo-Iranian Oil Company, but President Truman needed the support of the British in the Korean War. In the end, the British were persuaded to resume negotiations with the Iranians rather than to invade.

Almost everyone outside Iran saw the American response as very pro-Iranian, but the Mossadegh government denounced the United States for interfering in Iran's internal affairs. At the same time, Mossadegh wanted the United States to provide financial aid and buy Iranian oil in defiance of the British embargo[200].

The oil negotiations continued until late 1952. By then the British were willing to agree to nationalization and a 50-50 split of the profits, but Mossadegh killed the deal by demanding fifty million dollars in damages and lost profits.

When President Eisenhower came into office in January 1953, his administration reviewed the situation and concluded that Mossadegh was a likable man who meant well but was almost impossible to reason with. When he began threatening to sell oil rights to the Soviet Union, the Eisenhower administration decided he had to go.

The actual overthrow of Mossadegh was carried out by the CIA in August of 1953. It was controversial outside the United States, though most Americans at the time did not think much about it. America was fighting a Cold War against the worldwide spread of communism, and if Mossadegh was on the communist side in Iran, it was justifiable to get rid of him.

This point of view may seem a little naive, but few if any of the critics of the decision to overthrow Mossadegh have shown that it was unwise, viewed from the standpoint of American and Western European interests in 1953. Many of the criticisms focus on Iranian self-determination and do not take into account the larger framework in which the decision was made. The potential impact of Mossadegh's words and actions extended far beyond Iran's borders.

The containment policy started by President Truman and continued by President Eisenhower would have been badly weakened if the Soviet Union got control of Iran or its oil industry. This was one of the reasons why President Truman was prepared to send three Army divisions to Iran to drive the Soviets out by force.

When Mossadegh began moving Iran into the orbit of the Soviet Union, he had to go. For strategic reasons, the United States could not let the Soviet Union get control of Iran's oil.

President Eisenhower knew from his own experience that oil is essential for tank warfare. In 1953 many people in the United States and Europe were concerned that the Soviet Union wanted to invade Western Europe with tanks. Stalin added to these concerns by his threatening remarks and conduct. If the Soviet Union had gained control of the Iranian oil fields, it would have had a source of tank fuel that was outside Europe and almost impossible to cut off. The Germans did not cut this supply off during World War II, and they were stronger than any of the Western European armies were in 1953.

During World War II, the Soviets produced more tanks than the Germans, French, English, or Americans. Under the right conditions they could have produced enough tanks to overwhelm Western Europe. The British and French armies were small, West Germany had no army, East Germany was already under Russian control, and the American troops then in Europe would not have been enough to stop a major tank invasion. In addition, thousands of American troops were still tied down in Korea.

President Eisenhower had many things to consider in connection with the Mossadegh crisis. The Anglo-Iranian Oil Company was probably not a significant factor to him, compared to the lives and safety of the Western Europeans and the American soldiers defending them. The United States was thousands of miles away, and it would have taken too much time to transport tanks and soldiers to Europe to stop a Soviet invasion. It was vitally important to America to prevent the Soviets from gaining control of Iran and its oil fields.

President Eisenhower had a strong emotional commitment to the freedom and independence of Third World countries[201], and he was in favor of Iran's quest for freedom and autonomy. The primary motive for overthrowing Mossadegh was to prevent the Soviet Union from obtaining control of Iran's oil. He did not think Mossadegh was strong enough, healthy enough, or clever enough to prevent Iran from falling under the domination of the Soviet Union.

After Mossadegh was overthrown, the Shah's power was restored. He steered Iran away from Soviet domination by cultivating good relations with the United States and increasing his power within Iran as much as possible. This strategy worked reasonably well; he reigned for thirty-eight years, longer than any other Iranian ruler of the twentieth century.

President Eisenhower's successors, Presidents Kennedy, Johnson, Nixon, and Ford, did not intervene significantly in Iranian affairs. President Carter was a different story. He did nothing to prevent Khomeini from taking over, and Khomeini was easily able to defeat the few disorganized people that did stand up to him. Soon after that began a pivotal event in Iran-American relations, the Iranian hostage crisis of 1979.

The crisis began on Sunday, November 4, 1979, when hundreds of Iranians entered the United States Embassy in Tehran, seized everyone, and took them away as hostages. This was an invasion of American territory, and the Marines guarding the embassy were willing to fight the invaders to the death, but they were told not to resist. As a result, fifty-two Americans were held captive for 444 days[202]. None of them were killed or mutilated, but they were beaten, handcuffed, blindfolded, and subjected to death threats and cruel psychological tortures[203].

Within forty-eight hours Khomeini gave the kidnapping his official blessing and began to assert control over the kidnappers. The ostensible purpose of the kidnapping was to force President Carter to return the shah to Iran, so that Khomeini could torture him, put him on trial, and kill him. The shah was in America seeking medical treatment for terminal cancer.

The hostages were held against their will for 444 days, and all of President Carter's efforts to liberate them failed. They were not set free until after he left office.

The crisis caused great damage to America's reputation abroad and self-esteem at home. It occurred only a few years after the Vietnam War ended, and it was profoundly upsetting to Americans. It laid the groundwork for many terrorist acts of the 1980s and 1990s, by convincing terrorists that they could attack Americans with impunity.

After months of attempts to negotiate produced no results, President Carter authorized a rescue operation involving eight helicopters, but it failed miserably. There was no CIA intelligence to go on, and nobody to contact once they reached Tehran. Many anti-Khomeini Iranians would gladly have helped the escape effort, but the Carter administration had no communications with any of them.

A desert sandstorm disabled three of the helicopters, and several people were killed when another helicopter collided with a refueling plane. The operation was called off before they even got to Tehran, where the captives were being held. The Iranian government did not learn about the attempt until afterward. It then split the captives up, hiding them in different places so that nobody could rescue them in a similar operation in the future[204].

Some people believe that President Carter lost the 1980 presidential election because voter frustration over the hostage crisis gave Ronald Reagan the margin of victory. Whether or not this was true, the hostages were released immediately after President Reagan was sworn into office.

President Reagan did not know much about Iranian culture and probably did not spend much time trying to learn about it. His objective was to destroy the Soviet Union. His strategy was to denounce the Soviets and bankrupt them by forcing them to spend too much on military programs. He also wanted to reduce the influence of their client states such as Cuba and Nicaragua.

The Iranian government did not oppose these efforts, since a weakened Soviet Union would strengthen their influence. In addition, the Iraq-Iran war was going on, and Iran did not want a crisis with the United States at the same time.

President Reagan was convinced that the communist government in Nicaragua was going to allow terrorist groups to set up bases for training and attacks on the United States. He could not get Congress to share his conviction or give him funds to do something about it. He needed another source of money to finance the Contra rebels in their attempt to overthrow the Nicaraguan government.

Eventually the Iranian and American governments negotiated a deal. The Iranians paid cash for weapons and promised to set free some American hostages captured by Hezbollah in Lebanon. The hostages were not timely released, but the cash was delivered and the Americans used it to finance the Contras. Both sides benefited from this transaction, although President Reagan did have some problems when the Iran-Contra scandal arose in Congress. He weathered the storm and eventually saw the fruits of his labor: the collapse of the Soviet Union, the departure of the Soviet Army from Afghanistan, the fall of the Sandinista government, and the tearing down of the Berlin Wall.

Aside from Iran-Contra, President Reagan's main policy toward Iran was one of laissez faire. The Khomeini outlaw regime could do whatever it wanted, as long as American lives and property were not harmed. The Iranian government tested President Reagan in his second term by attacking oil tankers that were flying the American flag, and he responded with force. The U.S. navy sank several Iranian vessels and oil platforms. The Iranian government backed off, and things quieted down.

President Reagan never gave serious thought to overthrowing the Khomeini outlaw regime and replacing it with a democracy. His attention was focused heavily on the Soviet Union, and he wanted the mullahs to stop making trouble so he could remain focused on that.

President Reagan's successors, Presidents George H. W. Bush and Bill Clinton, were similarly inclined. As long as Iran's name was not associated with acts of terror against American citizens or property, it had little to fear from the United States.

The mullahs and ayatollahs in the Iranian government quickly learned to exploit this "turn a blind eye" attitude. For a long time, they were able to stay out of trouble by letting Hezbollah, or al Qaeda or some other group take the blame for terrorist acts. The groups were usually happy to do so, in the hope that it would help bring in donations and new members.

President George H. W. Bush attempted to improve relations with Iran at the beginning of his term in 1988, but Khomeini put an end to it by issuing a fatwa for the murder of Salman Rushdie, an Indian author whose book, *The Satanic Verses,* outraged Moslems all over the world. Soon President Bush became occupied with more urgent matters, such as the end of the Cold War, Saddam Hussein's invasion of Kuwait, and Operation Desert Storm.

President Bush was President Reagan's vice president during the Iran-Contra scandal, so he was more than a little cautious in dealing with the Iranian government. His administration succeeded in obtaining the release of the last surviving American hostages in Lebanon, but it took three years of negotiating. By that time many American politicians were angry with Iran for the murder of Lieutenant Colonel William Higgins in 1989[205] and the murder of Shahpour Bakhtiar in 1991. The final straw was Iran's persistent efforts to prevent the Israelis and Palestinians from negotiating a peace treaty. This removed any incentive to improve relations with the Iranian government.

President Clinton was the first Vietnam War protester to be elected president. He had a phobia of getting into any situations that could lead to warfare for fear that history would remember him as the president that got the United States into "another Vietnam". He did not want to risk military confrontations with belligerent governments such as the Iranian government, so he took no effective actions against Iran in response to the bombings of the Khobar Towers or the U. S. Embassies in Kenya and Tanzania.

The Khomeini insiders grew even bolder. They bought billions of dollars of weapons from Russia and China and began their nuclear weapons program in earnest.

President George W. Bush was in office when the Iran-al-Qaeda attack on the World Trade Center occurred. He concluded that a strong and effective response was called for. In his 2002 State of the Union address, he stated:

"We will be deliberate, yet time is not on our side. I will not wait on events while dangers gather. I will not stand by as peril draws closer and closer. The United States of America will not permit the world's most dangerous regimes to threaten us with the world's most destructive weapons."[206]

As of the end of 2004, President Bush has not taken any military action against Iran. However, he has publicized the evil deeds of the Iranian government and announced that he cannot let it acquire nuclear weapons on his watch. He has also criticized the Iranian government for a "lack of transparency," which means outsiders cannot see how it is operating and reaching its decisions.

The Bush administration considers lack of transparency dangerous, because it increases the risk of a war that might have been avoided.

The entry of China into the Korean War is an example. In 1950, the internal operations and motives of the Chinese and American governments were not transparent to each other. Neither of them could be confident they knew what the other was really after.

The result was that the Chinese intervened in the Korean War out of fear the United States planned to invade China. This forced both sides into a bitter and prolonged stalemate during which many lives were lost. After the war, America and China did not resume normal trade relations for twenty years. If the internal processes of the Chinese and American governments had been more transparent to each other, things would not have escalated to this point. Many American, Korean, and Chinese lives would have been saved, and China would have started on its path to wealth many years sooner.

The modern world cannot afford costly misunderstandings of this type, and the Bush administration is demanding more transparency from Iran's government. Without transparency, relatively innocent acts can cause suspicion and lead to excessive responses, which can lead to unnecessary conflict.

Besides demanding more transparency, what strategy should the United States pursue against Iran now? An armed invasion is unwise, unless something occurs that the Iranian people would see as reasonable grounds for sending in troops. Even in such a case, it would be difficult to persuade them not to rush to the defense of their government. The Iranian people have a fierce resistance to anything that resembles colonialism.

> Iranians are proud of having successfully resisted multiple attempts by covetous foreign powers to colonize or control our country. Our nation is vividly aware of its history, which has included invasions, wars, and frequent manipulations of our domestic affairs by external forces. To this day, our minds are heavily influenced by such experiences.[207]

Some people have argued that the United States should contact the more moderate members of the Iranian government and offer incentives to get them to stop supporting terrorism. Unfortunately, this approach does not work. France, Germany, and Great Britain have all tried it, and none of them had any success with it.

The Iranians are among the world's smoothest talkers, so when someone wants to negotiate with a seemingly moderate Iranian politician, they will provide one. But no matter what assurances are given the fundamental behavior of the Khomeini outlaw regime never changes. Examples of this are plentiful.

The Iranian government has never canceled Khomeini's death decree for Salman Rushdie. In February of 1998 Ayatollah Nateq-Nouri reaffirmed Khomeini's decree and expressed a strong desire for someone to kill Rushdie.[208]

> The Iranian government has never turned over to Germany the agents who killed four Kurdish activists at the Mykonos Restaurant in Berlin in 1992.

They have never turned over Imad Mugniyeh to the United States.

The Majlis members shouted, "Death to America!" after voting to continue enriching uranium.

They have never turned over to the United States any of the 350 or so al Qaeda terrorists they detained in 2003.

The Majlis played no part in deciding whether Iran should pursue ballistic missile and nuclear weapons programs.

They have never apologized for Khomeini's 1984 disruption of the Hajj to Mecca with anti-American demonstrations. Khomeini ordered the Iranian pilgrims to demonstrate, and more than 400 pilgrims died in the fighting[209]. Since then the Saudi government has given in and now allows anti-American demonstrations during the Hajj, as long as it is kept low profile.

Many Westerners seem to believe that because Khatami likes rock and roll and Rafsanjani supports free market reforms, they are moderates. Khamenei, who dislikes such things, is seen as the hardliner. But in reality these men are all part of the same small group pursuing the same basic goals. They all want to destroy the American, European, and Israeli civilizations. They all want to control the oil fields of Iraq, Kuwait, and Saudi Arabia. Some smile, some snarl, but in their hearts they are all the same.

Rafsanjani's remark that an atomic bomb could completely destroy Israel, while a similar bomb would "merely do damage" to the surrounding Islamic countries is a chilling reminder of how dangerous the Iranian government has become. The Iranian government's main excuse for hostility to Israel has been the treatment of the Palestinians, and yet Rafsanjani is willing to kill them all in order to strike at Jewish people.

The Khomeini outlaw regime must end, not only because the Iranian people want them out, but also because the safety and welfare of the United States and the world require it. The best way to overthrow the Khomeini outlaw regime is for the Iranian people themselves to do it, but if the United States is forced into action before then, what is the best way to present it to the Iranian public?

If that fateful day ever comes, the following points can be made:

First, the United States respects Iran's right to rule itself and will leave when our goals have been met. The Iranians are tired of centuries of meddling by foreigners. It is important to stress that America is interested only in securing the protections we need before turning control over to an elected Iranian government. Our track records in Iraq, Afghanistan, Germany, and Japan would be a strong point in our favor on this issue. They show that we do let people run their own countries as soon as they are able to do so.

Second, Iran can keep its nuclear weapons once adequate safeguards are in place and a democratically elected government is running the country. This tells the Iranians that we trust them to be as mature and responsible with nuclear weapons as the Indians, Pakistanis, Chinese, Russians, and Israelis. If this point is not made, we will have insulted them by implying that they are not as trustworthy and reliable as these other people.

This point would be tremendously controversial in the United States, but if the Iranians see the United States president taking heat for insisting upon this, and standing firm, it will be a strong boost to his credibility. If the French and German governments attack the president for this, they will have insulted the Iranians and portrayed themselves as neo-colonialists. If the French and German governments support the president, it will be harder for other countries and the media to attack him effectively.

Third, America will help Iran rebuild if the Iranians want us to. One of the reasons the overwhelming majority of Iraqis cooperated with the American occupation was that we rebuilt a tremendous number of schools, hospitals, and other buildings. We also restored electrical services to a better level than before. Like Cyrus the Great 2,500 years earlier, we did more for the Iraqis than their own ruler. We can do the same for Iran as well.

The prospects for trade, commerce, and tourism with a rebuilt Iran would be mutually beneficial. Many Iranian-Americans would work hard to promote this, using the skills they have learned in America and their understanding of both cultures. The vast majority of young Iranians who are unemployed or underemployed would jump at the chance to have paying jobs.

The Iranian people have a lot to offer the world, and all they need is to change their form of government. If they are convinced that the United States will support them, no mullah on earth can stop them.

Chapter 14

The Mullahs are Incompetent Leaders

There are a number of things a free and democratic Iran could use American help with, if they chose to accept it. The mullahs of the Khomeini outlaw regime have proven that they are incompetent at running Iran's government or economic affairs, and a lot of repair work is needed.

Iran's educational system has not kept pace. Every year about 1,500,000 high school graduates compete for 85,000 places in colleges. For those who get into college, about one in twenty-three finds a decent job after graduating[210]. That amounts to less than one fourth of one percent of all high school graduates getting a college degree and a good job four years later. More than ninety-nine percent of them wind up unemployed or in jobs below their capacity, with limited opportunities for advancement.

The Iranian government has also mismanaged the oil industry, which is where most of Iran's foreign currency comes from. Oil production is about half what it was before Khomeini took over, even though Iran's oil fields are enormous. The mullahs have made an estimated 300 billion dollars from oil in the last twenty-two years,[211] but instead of maintaining and upgrading their oil fields and equipment, they have squandered it buying weapons and uranium from China[212], missiles from North Korea[213], and missile technology from Russia[214].

Many Iranian oil experts say that the immediate need for investment in the oil and gas industry is . . . a minimum of 100 billion dollars over the next decade.[215]

Despite these vast oil fields, the Khomeini government actually imports gasoline! Iran's refineries produce about 8.45 million gallons of gasoline (32 million liters) a day, but Iran consumes about 17.43 million gallons a day (66 million liters), so they have to import the remaining 8.98 million gallons (34 million liters)[216]. The shortfall costs them billions of dollars a year at current oil prices, and the prices are likely to go higher in the future.

In short, the mullahs are so inept that if gasoline prices go up, Iran loses money. A price increase of one dollar a gallon would cost the Iranian government $540,000 a day.

America and Europe have private oil companies that could help a democratic Iranian government solve this problem. The resulting income stream could also be used for other public works that would create construction jobs, such as roads, hospitals, and schools. All that stands in the way is the Iranian government.

Iran has entered into a memorandum of understanding with a Chinese oil company to develop the Yadavaran oil field and build a liquefied natural gas refinery[217]. However, the Chinese company does not have the technology needed to do the work[218]. It will have to either steal the technology or bring in other companies to supply it. The Iranians could have done this work themselves, without sharing profits, simply by using their oil revenues to hire the outside companies to build these facilities. But the funds were not there, because they were spent elsewhere.

In the meantime, Rafsanjani has invested billions of dollars in Canada. At the time, the Canadians were so grateful that some of them wanted to name a freeway after him. They did not seem to realize how easily the income from these investments could be used to fund terrorist operations against Canada and the United States. Hezbollah and al Qaeda already have people in Canada, and Rafsanjani is already involved in all the assassinations and bombings the Iranian government sponsors.

The runaway military spending of the Khomeini outlaw regime is another long term problem that has seriously crippled the economy. Iran has better things to spend its money on, like housing, education, pensions for war veterans, and the construction of the longest canal in the world, from the Caspian Sea to the Indian Ocean. Every dollar spent on guns, missiles, uranium, or plutonium is a dollar less for these types of projects, which would benefit the country far more.

The Khomeini habit of military overspending, combined with wasteful subsidies within Iran, makes it essential to attract foreign investments to develop the infrastructure. As of 2004, the Majlis is headed in the opposite direction, passing laws that make it harder for foreign companies to make money by helping Iran.

The most recent legislation would require foreign companies to get approval from the Majlis as well as the executive branch of government. Instead of bribing a few key figures, foreign companies would have to bribe some or all of the Majlis, which has more than 250 members. If each member wanted one tenth of what Rafsanjani's son was promised by Statoil (i.e., $1.5 million), the total bribe cost for the Majlis alone would be $375,000,000! There are very few foreign investors who can afford this kind of expense on top of the startup costs for a project.

The economic incompetence of the Khomeini outlaw regime does even more damage to the Iranian economy than the greed of the Majlis or the money the ayatollahs send out of the country. Khomeini was an economic illiterate who paid little attention to whether his laws and policies were hurting business or destroying jobs. At the beginning of his reign, oil production was less than one fourth of what it had been under the shah, but Khomeini did not care. Restoring oil productivity was a low priority for him.

When negotiations for selling natural gas to the Russians bogged down, Khomeini cut off all natural gas sales to them, resulting in a loss estimated at $100,000,000 a year. He did not care how much damage that did or how many jobs were lost. He is famous for saying that his revolution was not about the price of watermelons.

Khomeini's successors are just as inept at economic and business policy, although they care more about money. The Rafsanjani clan is involved in copper mining, television, pistachio exporting, oil, public construction projects, an auto assembly plant, and an airline company[219]. For a long time Khamenei received twenty percent of the profits on every car sold in Iran, ostensibly for "charity". This practice has allegedly stopped now[220].

Iran's productivity is far less than it was under the Pahlavi dynasty. One commentator has listed a number of problems attributable to the Khomeini outlaw regime's ignorance of economics and business:

Government dominating the economy,

Little or no private sector participation,

Low productivity of workers,

Old manufacturing equipment,

Low quality products,

Bureaucratic regulation,

Doubts about the future stability of the country, and

Slow pace of privatization of public companies[221].

The Khomeini outlaw regime controls about eighty percent of the economy and bases its long-range planning on Five-Year Plans. They are currently operating under the Third Five-Year Plan, covering the period from March 20, 2000, to March 20, 2005[222]. Khatami prepared it but was careful to get approval from Khamenei before submitting it to the Majlis for approval[223].

The Five-Year Plans were a famous feature of Soviet and Communist Chinese governments of the past. Stalin had them, Khrushchev had them, Mao had them. They set ambitious goals for all kinds of things. But their most distinctive feature was that they didn't work! They never improved the standard of living, and only rarely did they strengthen the economy or government.

This should not be taken to imply that Iran under the Khomeini outlaw regime closely resembles Stalin's Soviet Union or Mao's China. Many Iranian observers see it as more closely resembling its surviving partner in the "Axis of Evil," North Korea.

Sazman-e Mojahedin-e Enghleab-e Eslami, . . . an influential group in the reformist camp, has said that contrary to their expectations about conservatives [i.e., Khomeini outlaw regime supporters] adopting a Chinese style of development (expanding socioeconomic freedoms and limiting political activities), so far they've shown that they are interested in a North Korean style of running the country in which all sort of freedoms would be pushed to a minimum.

As a matter of fact, almost everybody was predicting that model, because in the past couple of years, the conservatives have talked about it all the time[224].

The earliest Five-Year Plans were drafted by the Soviet Union during the 1930s[225]. But they didn't work. Over three million people starved to death in the winter of 1933 alone.

Khatami's Third Five-Year Plan assumes that Iran will reduce unemployment among young people by creating 900,000 new jobs each year.

To create this many jobs, Iran would need foreign businesses to make huge investments in Iran. But the Majlis is driving them away. The Majlis recently rejected a proposal by Turkcell Iletisim Hizmetleri, Turkey's largest cell phone company, to dramatically increase the availability of cell phones in Iran. This would have created new sales jobs for young people, just as the Verizon stores have in many American communities.

The Majlis has also delayed the opening of Khomeini International Airport. One of the contractors is a Turkish company, and they claim that somehow that would enable Israel to spy on the airport. This is preposterous considering that Iran and Turkey have entered into many joint projects relating to commerce, energy, and other areas of mutual interest.

Khatami's Five-Year Plans tend to rely heavily on projected investments by foreigners, so when the Majlis drives the foreigners away, it is virtually guaranteed that the plan goals will not be met.

The Iranian government controls about eighty percent of the economy[226], so when a Five-Year Plan, or one of the yearly budgets within the plan, goes haywire, the effect is much more powerful than in a democracy where private industry makes up a much larger portion of the economy.

Khatami's Fourth Five-Year Plan for March 20, 2005 to March 20, 2010, relies heavily on higher oil prices and projects eleven billion dollars of foreign investments. The Iranian government is trying to encourage investment by Asian countries, which buy ninety percent of Iran's oil exports[227]. However, Iran exported less than half of the oil it produced as of March 2004 ($1.2 billion out of $2.7 billion total[228]), so it is doubtful that relying heavily on oil revenues will work that well in the future.

With the Majlis driving foreign investors away, it will be difficult to bring in that much from foreign countries unless Iran invades one and manages to loot it for eleven billion dollars more than the cost of the invasion. That would be much easier for them to contemplate if there were no American troops in Iraq (vast oil deposits) or Afghanistan (vast gold and mineral deposits, opium farms, and vineyards with cancer-fighting grapes).

Iran currently has oil export revenues of $1.2 billion, which are relatively small in light of the demand for oil and the size of their oil deposits. It is only twice what Iran made last year exporting Persian rugs. The rug makers had a good year[229], but that simply highlights the Iranian government's mishandling of the oil industry.

The Iranian telecommunications industry is another example of how the Khomeini outlaw regime gets in the way of economic growth and progress. The Third Five-Year Plan called for sixteen million telephone lines by 2005, but the equipment manufactured in Iran is outdated and has a lower capacity for transmission and switching than the current international standards[230]. The telephone cables in Tehran are too old to provide good Internet access[231].

The obvious answer is to allow foreign companies to provide modern equipment and infrastructure. But the Iranian government will not allow this. As a result, the Iranian telecommunications industry is developing too slowly to meet popular demand.

Internet expansion is also impaired by government censorship. Government agents have arrested web technicians, gotten their passwords, then seized or erased computer hard drives. Protests have been lodged with Vice President Mohammad Ali Abtahi[232], but to no avail. The Iranian government is now torturing Internet authors and editors in order to obtain written confessions of crimes they did not commit[233].

In the meantime, millions of Iranian youth cannot find jobs. Many of them turn to drugs. It is a tragic waste of lives and human resources, all to please a small group of tired old men whose usefulness to their country ended a long time ago. The British have gone, the Russians have gone, and now it is time for the clerics to go. Most Iranians want to be in the forefront of human evolution, not the rear guard.

Iran has been waiting too long for the good times, and the mullahs should not be allowed to delay them any longer. Their time has gone, and they must go too, the sooner the better.

Chapter 15

An Alternative to the Khomeini Outlaw Regime

The mullahs have tried to convince Iranians that there are no alternatives to the Khomeini outlaw regime. But there are. One such alternative is Reza Shah Pahlavi II, the son of the shah who went into exile in 1979. Reza Pahlavi is currently living in exile in the United States. This was not by choice. When his father left Iran in 1979, he went with him to avoid certain death at the hands of Khomeini.

After his father died in 1980, Reza Pahlavi went to college in the United States and graduated from the University of Southern California with a degree in political science. After studying all forms of government, he concluded that democracy would be the best choice for Iran.

His primary goal is to turn Iran into a secular democracy[234]. He has made a point of getting to know a wide diversity of Iranian opposition groups, including members of the clergy who favor democracy and the separation of government and religion. He feels that all the pro-democracy groups should work together for the sake of Iran, and he has worked hard to set an example of this.

He is devoted to promoting an Iranian democracy with leaders elected by the people. He has been very influential in spreading this belief, through his connections with Iranian baby boomers and the sixty percent of Iranian youth who are from his generation.

Reza Pahlavi, the Crown Prince of Iran, who lives in exile in the United States with his family.

In 2001 he began broadcasting in Farsi into Iran, discussing the desires and frustrations Iranians were facing, particularly the younger generation. After 9/11 he became very well known and now has a following large enough to worry the Iranian government. One Iranian has described his message by saying, "When he says we just want to be normal again, this touches everybody. Our society has decided to become a secular democracy."[235]

He recently demonstrated his feelings for Iran when he intervened in the National Geographic Society controversy over a map which labeled the Persian Gulf as the Arabic Sea. Arabs were in favor of the name change, while Iranians vigorously objected to changing a name that has stood for centuries.

Rather than picketing or calling for boycotts, Mr. Pahlavi met with the president of the National Geographic Society to discuss the situation. The meeting was held on December 4, 2004, and afterward Mr. Pahlavi announced, "I am pleased to have been reassured that the National Geographic Society recognizes "Persian Gulf" as the undisputed historic name of the body of water south of the Iranian plateau."[236]. This is a good example of his leadership style, which involves timely interventions in a diplomatic manner that is usually more effective than confrontation and denunciation.

Reza Pahlavi meeting with the president of the National Geographic Society

If the Iranian people keep an open mind they will look past his royal heritage and see an Iranian citizen who loves his country and wants to help improve it. He should have the same right to run for public office as any other Iranian or Iranian-American.

He cannot do this without first eliminating the Khomeini outlaw government, however. They hate him and the entire Pahlavi family with an animosity so deep that they would rather destroy the country than allow the people to vote for him. This hatred is due in part to a strong feeling of insecurity, and their feeling of insecurity is mostly justified.

The Pahlavi dynasty changed the face of Iran, creating a solid industrial base and an economic middle class for the first time in history. The Khomeini outlaw regime has squandered a tremendous portion of what it received in 1979, and the mullahs have no idea how to rebuild what they have lost.

Reza Pahlavi has a lot of support in Iran, but his supporters remain silent for fear of being murdered. He has similarly learned to live with the fear that assassins could attack at any time, and this has given him a heightened degree of empathy with Iranians from all walks of life.

He reaches out to those Iranian youth who feel disenfranchised. Most of these youth are unemployed or underemployed, and many of them pass the time using cheap drugs. They have no alternatives under the Khomeini outlaw regime, and he is one of the few leaders to give them hope for getting good jobs under a democratic government.

His ability to communicate has been greatly enhanced by the Internet and satellite television. The Iranian government has arrested and fined people for owning such things, but his popularity continues to grow.

Chapter 16

The Iranian People Want Democracy

One of the best things that the Pahlavi dynasty did for ordinary Iranian people was to encourage pride and high expectations for themselves and their children. Education and hard work were stressed as keys to success. These attitudes became widespread, and most of the Iranians who came to the United States had them. They expected to succeed as long as they tried to assimilate and worked hard. And as a group Iranians did succeed here. This is partly because they were attracted by the traditional American attitude toward success, exemplified by statements such as:

> Our system is based on freedom and unlimited opportunity for anyone willing to work hard to achieve his or her dreams. You can win if you are determined and make up your mind to succeed. It doesn't matter who you are, what you look like, or where you come from, you can do it.[237].

Research has shown that optimistic people tend to be more successful than pessimists. They are less bothered by temporary setbacks, they have more self-confidence, and they live longer.

As of 2003, more than eighty percent of Iranian-Americans speak fluent English. More than seventy-five percent of them work in technical, professional, managerial, or administrative positions. The percentage of Iranian-Americans with Ph.D.s is six times the national average. Their average household income is about twenty percent

Twenty-first century student protesters in Tehran.

above the national average[238]. More than ninety percent of them own their own homes. Almost none of them are homeless.

Iranians love the United States, and more of them have emigrated to the United States than any other country. One private organization estimates that about 1,500,000 Iranians have come to America. The next most popular countries are Turkey, Iraq, and the United Arab Emirates, all of which are very close to Iran[239].

To go from immigrant to homeowner in one or two generations is impressive, and it is clear that collectively Iranian-Americans have been a tremendous success story. They have worked hard and have had their labors rewarded.

At the same time, most of them have kept in contact with relatives in Iran. Thus for the past twenty-five years, people living in Iran have been hearing how things work in America and how it is possible to make money and live well there. At the same time, they have endured tremendous oppression in Iran: the hardships and deaths during the Iran-Iraq War, the constant harassment, arrests and torture by the Iranian government, the severe limits on their ability to find good jobs or start new businesses, the shortages of food and resources, and the many other unpleasant aspects of life under the Khomeini outlaw regime.

It is only natural that intelligent Iranians, hearing about the blessings and opportunities that freedom brings, want to live in freedom and elect their own rulers. Many of them are convinced that if the Americans can elect their own rulers, so can the Iranians. And this is of course true.

This man set himself on fire after Malaysia denied him asylum and said it would return him to Iran.

In addition, the Iranians have a great deal of pride, and people who take pride in themselves do not want to be seen as falling behind. It is only human to compare ourselves with others. For example, research suggests that most people would be happier earning $70,000 a year when their neighbors are earning $60,000, than earning $80,000 a year when their neighbors are earning $90,000[240]. The extra $10,000 is less satisfying than knowing that they are outperforming their neighbors.

In the areas of democracy, prosperity, and human rights, Iran has fallen behind many of its neighbors. This is a significant change from the past.

In the early 1970s Iran was wealthy, powerful, influential, and far ahead of its neighbors. It was a country that others looked up to and often envied. College education for women is a good example. Nobody except the shah of Iran and the King of Afghanistan supported it. In the rest of the countries in the region, very few women went to college.

Thirty years later the story is different. Women still go to college, but government policy limits what they can do after they graduate. Iran has taken several steps backward in human rights. Its leaders tried to return Iran to the lifestyle of 1400 years ago, but it did not work. The Koran offers little guidance on things that were not around in the time of the Prophet Mohammad, such as heroin, computers, satellite TV dishes, fast cars, women's bicycles[241], air pollution, and post-traumatic stress disorder.

Iran's neighbors are changing rapidly. The Iraqis are free of Saddam Hussein and moving rapidly toward elected leaders, voting rights, and a mandate for decent treatment for all races and tribes. Afghanistan has held the first presidential election in its history, which the Afghanis themselves trace back over five thousand years. The first ballot was cast by a woman.

India has been a democracy for more than fifty years, and Pakistan is headed in that direction as well. Some of the former Soviet republics of Central Asia are also moving toward democracy.

Many Iranians cannot help feeling a little embarrassed that so many of their neighbors are rushing past them toward democracy. It used to be that Iran was rushing past them.

It is particularly irritating to think that Afghanistan is pulling ahead of them. Iran has more than four times as many people, a higher literacy rate, and far more wealth than Afghanistan. Yet everyone in Afghanistan that wanted to run for president was allowed to.

Most Iranians are confident that the country is ready for democracy. Their ancestors had a constitutional monarchy from 1906 to 1911, when no other country in the area was even thinking about it. They already have experience with political parties and elections. The problem is that only members of the Khomeini outlaw regime can run or hold office. A sizable number of politicians held office once but were not allowed to run for a second term.

There have been similar problems with the Majlis, where 285 of the seats are reserved for Moslems only. Only four seats are reserved for people of other religions: one for a Jew, one for a Zoroastrian, and two for Eastern Orthodox Christians[242]. Bahais, Buddhists, Hindus, Catholics, Protestants, and atheists are out of luck.

After the 9/11 tragedy, many Iranians demonstrated in favor of the United States and democracy, and thousands of them went to jail for it[243]. Demonstrations have occurred since then, and they seem to be becoming less predictable.

On September 26, 2004, demonstrations occurred in Tehran and several other cities even though the Iranian government had not committed any widely known atrocities.

Students booing Khatami during a speech at Tehran University in 2004.

The demonstrations occurred at the urging of a TV personality, Ahura Pirouz Khaleqi Yadzi[244], who broadcasts from California[245]. He made grandiose predictions that the Khomeini outlaw regime would fall on October 1 and promised to lead charter planes of Iranian expatriates back to Iran to restore order. The police did not harass the demonstrators and virtually no fighting occurred. Many of the people there said that they did not take "Dr. Ahura" literally, but went to the demonstration to see what was going to happen[246].

> "That so many people come out on the invitation of a man who was the center of jokes and laughter for the last two or three months tells you about the depth of the hate the Iranians have for the ruling ayatollahs. It also showed that the society, frustrated, humiliated, oppressed, and insulted by the clerics, has reached the explosion point. It is also dangerous, for it shows that *any group, or a hostile nation with proper planning and program, might bring down the Islamic Republic,*" one Iranian journalist told the Persian service of Radio France International[247]. [emphasis added]

> For Dr. Mohammad-Reza Djalili, a professor at the Graduate Institute of International Studies of Geneva, Switzerland, "this shows that people are awaiting a messiah to liberate them from this regime and for this reason, they accept any sign."

> In his view, as well as that of a journalist in Tehran, since the reforms promised by the President Mohammad Khatami have all failed, "people are despaired [sic], grabbing on [to] anything to salvage themselves, ready to pay the highest price."[248]

The Iranian people are tired of the Khomeini outlaw regime. As one filmmaker said, on a different occasion, "The Afghans and the

Iraqis have been freed from dictatorships, why not us?"[249] Another Iranian, an architect, told an interviewer,

> "... there isn't any difference between reformers and the conservatives anymore. ... It is simple. We don't want the Islamic Republic anymore. It took us a quarter of a century to realize that the revolution has ended in failure."[250]

Protester at a Rafsanjani speech in 2004.

The average Iranian believes, like the average American, that it is insane to put people in jail for owning satellite TV dishes, videotapes, cassette tapes, Bibles[251], women's bicycles, cosmetics, or sexy clothing. They know that you can own such things without compromising your religious values. Most of them know that Americans have no interest in manipulating Iran's government the way the British and Russians did for so many years. The thought of selling Iranian oil to Americans does not bother them. American oil companies offered much better deals fifty years ago, and they may well today.

> "We are willing to exchange the war on terrorism and the fight for cheaper oil for a more democratically elected government in Iran," said Shayan Arya, president of the Seattle chapter of the Constitutionalist Party of Iran, which organized the demonstration of Iranian-Americans in support of the United States policy on Iraq[252].

It is time for the Khomeini outlaw regime to be replaced by officials elected by the people, not imposed from above. The United States can play a role by facilitating this transition. If the Iranian people are provided with the tools and support they need, they can and will do the job. They will complete the move toward democracy that their ancestors began 100 years ago.

The Khomeini outlaw regime has become too dangerous for the Iranian people or the world to tolerate much longer. They must give up power, so that other people can take over, people who are more in tune with the Iranian public. Iran's independence is well established, and there is no need for more killing, torture, or mass graves. Until the Khomeini outlaw regime is out of power, Iranian citizens cannot begin their own search for the mass graves that already exist.

September 18, 2001 08:30 PM   Tehran, Mohseni Sq.   Tehran24.com

Iranians in Tehran holding a pro-American candlelight vigil after 9/11.

Chapter 17

Why Iran Must Become a Nuclear Democracy

There are countries with nuclear weapons on three sides of Iran. To the east, India, China, and Pakistan have them. To the north is Russia, and to the west Israel.

Nobody has made a serious effort to take away the nuclear weapons of these countries, and they are not likely to give them up voluntarily. Iran will be the same. Iranians feel that they are at least as stable and trustworthy as their neighbors when it comes to handling atomic bombs and nuclear missiles. Iran also has fewer people than all of these countries except Israel. Their army would be outnumbered in the event of a war.

Given these facts, we can predict how the Iranian people would feel about attempts by other countries to deprive them of nuclear weapons. A tiny percentage would favor unilateral disarmament and everyone else would reject the notion. Likely responses include:

Everyone else has them, why shouldn't we?

China and India have never used their nuclear weapons, why do you think we would use ours?

You didn't complain when Israel got their nuclear weapons, and they're much more volatile than we are. Why do you want to take away ours and let Israel keep theirs?

We're outnumbered by several countries with strong armies. We need our nuclear weapons as a deterrent[253].

Why don't you get rid of yours first? America has the most powerful conventional army in the world already.

These arguments are not being made by the current Iranian government because it denies that it is building nuclear weapons. It claims that it is developing nuclear power plants and other peaceful uses for radioactive materials. It even claims that nuclear weapons are unIslamic.

President Bush has rejected this story vigorously, pointing out that Iran does not need nuclear power because of its enormous oil and gas reserves. He has further pointed out that the natural gas Iran burns off during the refining process is worth more money than it would cost to build a nuclear facility, so if they were after cheap power, they would use natural gas, as many other countries do.

No matter what kind of government Iran has, it is going to be a nuclear power very soon.

Invading Iran for the stated purpose of stopping their nuclear weapons program would be a mistake. It would annoy and offend the Iranian people and almost certainly cause them to unite behind the mullahs. When a country is attacked, the people usually rally behind their government, even if they despise it during normal times.

Since we cannot prevent Iran from becoming a nuclear power, our best hope is for Iran to become a democracy, so that its leaders pay attention to public opinion and take it into account in deciding their actions and policies. They must also keep their nuclear weapons secure, so that terrorists and criminals have no access to them.

Three of the first five countries to acquire nuclear weapons were democracies: the United States, Britain, and France. The other two were Communist oligarchies, some would say dictatorships. All five of them have managed their political and military affairs in such a way as to avoid using their nuclear weapons in warfare. The risk of mutually assured destruction encouraged communist and non-communist nations to become more tolerant of each other and more cooperative in matters of mutual interest.

The mature members of the nuclear club have refrained from threats to use their nuclear weapons against each other. When two of the younger nuclear countries, India and Pakistan, began to threaten each other, the mature members helped dissuade them and to find less dangerous ways to assert their national pride. If the mullahs had been one of the two warring parties, a peaceful resolution would not have occurred. They would have attacked the other party verbally, stepped up terrorist activities, and then accused it of dealing in bad faith.

The nuclear weapons situation furnishes another reason why it is in the best interests of the United States to support democracy in Iran. The Iranian people tend to be peace-loving, and the older ones still remember the horrors of the war with Iraq. The younger Iranians, like young people almost everywhere, are much more interested in enjoying life than in harming anyone. They are tired of living like prisoners. They want to live normal lives, like people in many other countries.

Michael Ledeen, a scholar at the American Enterprise Institute, said, "The Iranian people are probably the most enthusiastically pro-American people in the Islamic world."[254]. We need to encourage that attitude by helping them restore their freedom, democracy, and happiness. All they need from us is equipment, training, planning, support services, and possibly interim financing. Give them the means to win, and they will do the rest.

Chapter 18

The Solution to the Problem is Democracy

If Iran is going to develop and keep nuclear weapons, she owes it to the world to become a democracy. And America owes to Iran to help pay this debt. Democracy is the solution to the Iranian nuclear weapons problem. We cannot take the nukes away from the mullahs, because they are so rich that they can buy new ones or hire nuclear engineers to make them.

Instead, we must reduce the threat of Iranian nuclear weapons by helping the Iranian people create the secular democracy the majority of them want. They know that the Khomeini experiment has failed, and they are ready to move on. They will help us solve the nuclear problem if we help them solve their problem in obtaining freedom and a representative government.

Given that Iran would then become a nuclear democracy, it is fair to ask, Are the Iranians ready for democracy?

The historical evidence suggests that they are. Some of the evidence is:

In 1906, the Iranians succeeded in establishing the Majlis and defended it vigorously for five years, until the Russians invaded and destroyed it.

The Majlis provided for membership diversity by setting aside seats for several different minority religions.

The Majlis was able to debate, reach decisions, and formulate plans of action to carry out those decisions.

The Majlis struggled to eliminate foreign debt, rebuild the treasury, and promote economic self-sufficiency.

W. Morgan Shuster, the first American-born treasurer of Persia, observed the Majlis of 1911 in action and felt that it did reflect the desires and aspirations of the people it represented.

> We should make allowance for lack of technical knowledge; for the important question, of course, is that the Medjlis in the main represented the new and just ideals and aspirations of the Persian people. Its members were men of more than average education; some displayed remarkable talents and courage. Nearly all believed that the salvation of their country depended upon their efforts to place the constitutional government upon a firm and lasting basis, and that by such means alone would they be able to restore peace, order and prosperity, and check both the sale of their country to foreigners and the future political encroachments of Russia and England. . . .

> No Parliament can be rightly termed incompetent when it has the support of an entire people, when it recognizes its own limitations, and when its members are willing to undergo great sacrifices for their nation's dignity and sovereign rights.

> The Medjlis stood for an honest and progressive administration of Persia's affairs. On the day that this body was destroyed, with the connivance of the foreign powers, the last hope of honest or representative government in Persia disappeared. The Persian people refused to acquiesce in the coup d'etat which snuffed out the Medjlis, because they recognized that with it went their liberties, their rights, their nationality, and their future as an independent state[255].

Shuster's observations about the characteristics of the Persian people at that time are also worth noting.

> The Persians are as a rule kind and hospitable . . . They, or at least certain elements among them which had the support of the masses, proved their capacity to assimilate western civilization and ideas. They changed despotism into democracy in the face of

untold obstacles. Opportunities were equalized to such a degree that any man of ability could occupy the highest official posts. As a race they showed during the past five years an unparalleled eagerness for education. Hundreds of schools were established during the Constitutional regime. A remarkable free press sprang up over night, and fearless writers came forward . . . The Persians were anxious to adopt wholesale the political, ethical, and business codes of the most modern and progressive nations.[256].

The Persians of Shuster's day were eager for democracy, and they were willing to take advice from other people with more experience at democracy. They would have built a permanent constitutional democracy if the Russians under Czar Nicholas II had not destroyed it. The British were less obvious about it, but they too opposed a strong Persian legislature and did what they could to promote a weak shah and cheap oil. It is much easier to bribe, intimidate, or coerce one man than eighty.

After the Russians shut down the Majlis in 1911, democracy in Persia went underground. In the 1970s, Shah Reza II began introducing some rights and freedoms found in democracies, such as freedom of the press and freedom of speech, but he retained most of his power until the day he resigned and left Iran for good.

Democracy under the Khomeini outlaw regime has been nonexistent. Khomeini tried to create the appearance of democracy, and at first there was a variety of candidates and parties in the Majlis. But once his grip on power was strong, everyone except his supporters was frozen out of politics. The Council of Guardians simply kept their names off the ballot.

Democracy may have been dormant in Iran, but it has never been forgotten. Countless newspapers and magazines have tackled difficult and controversial subjects, even at the risk of imprisonment and death. Many teachers, professionals, and dissident ayatollahs have criticized the Iranian government and its practices, even at the risk of their own lives and well being. And during the last quarter century, the calls for a truly representative government have never ceased.

The present Iranian government is based on Khomeini's teachings, which are incompatible with democracy, Zoroastrianism, or traditional Islam. The primary rule in Khomeini's system is that whatever Khomeini says or does is right, perfect, and more important than any Islamic principles it conflicts with, even daily prayers, pilgrimage to Mecca, and the other pillars of Islam.

The secondary rule is that you should not worry if Khomeini's orders make no sense or appear to violate Islam. That is due to your limited and flawed intelligence and understanding, not to any defect in Khomeini. Ordinary people cannot expect to understand him completely.

Fortunately, most Iranians were too sensible to be fooled by Khomeini for long. Too many of his orders were stupid or cruel. An obvious example would be his decree mandating the rape of all virgins in prison before executing them. A less gruesome example would be his decree forbidding the game of chess. After Khomeini's death, his admirers attempted to institute bans of their own, on such things as dogs, satellite dishes, and women's bicycles.

Many devout Moslems around the world view Khomeini as a heretic, idolater, and blasphemer, but it is rare for them to publicly say so for fear of being killed. These Moslems will be secretly pleased if the Khomeini outlaw regime is replaced with a democratic government chosen by the Iranian people. Most of them would appreciate America's help in that effort, once they realized we were not going to exploit Iran the way the European powers did. They may not praise America openly, particularly if they are dependent on loans or trade concessions from France or Germany, but they will view the United States more kindly than before.

The longing of the Iranian people for democracy has been kept alive not only by Khomeini's heresies but also by contact with Iranians living in the United States and Canada. Through them many people in Iran have become familiar with how much better things are in the West.

In addition, the Iranians of today are better educated than their ancestors of ninety years ago. There were no colleges or universities then, but the Pahlavi rulers built many of them, and the Khomeini outlaw regime refrained from destroying them. Khomeini did shut down all the universities for a few years, but once the old curriculum had

Shayad Square, renamed Freedom Square after Khomeini destroyed all traces of freedom.

been replaced with Khomeini-oriented teachings, the schools were reopened.

Modern Iranians also have access to books, newspapers, tapes, and the Internet, which has broadened their horizons considerably. They know what is going on in other countries and how democracies conduct themselves. They are aware that in the United States, political demonstrations take place in which nobody is beaten up by the police or shot by a private militia.

Iranians are ready for democracy. They have wanted it for many years, they have seen that other people can make it work, and they have noticed that many of the wealthiest economies in the world are found in democratic places, such as France, the United States, Great Britain, California, and Florida. They know that Germany and Japan converted to democracy and became prosperous, peaceful countries. They can see the difference in standard of living between North Korea (insolvent dictatorship) and South Korea (prosperous democracy), where both populations belong to the same ethnic group.

Today's Iranians are better prepared for democracy than some of the other peoples who have succeeded at it. They have more examples to study, and they are already familiar with some of the issues. The Khomeini outlaw regime has tried to present the appearance of democracy without the substance, but in the process some Iranians have become familiar with the forms and features of democracy, such as parliamentary procedure and Supreme Court review of all death sentences.

The Iranians have won their battle for independence and freedom from British and Russian influence, and now it is time for them to win the battle for democracy.

We Americans have been entrusted with the sacred honor and privilege of supplying the Iranian people with the tools they need to convince the Khomeini outlaw regime to step down—and to take their country back by force if necessary. The rewards for both countries will be considerable. As Americans we can and must do it because it is only right and just.

Appendix A

Maps of Iran and a Few Nuclear Facilities

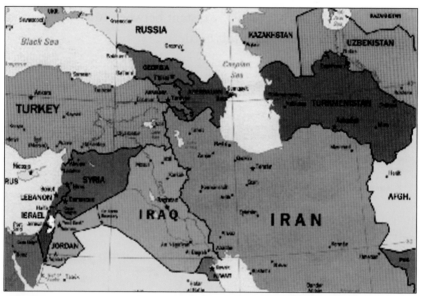

For the complete version of this map, go to
http://www.lib.utexas.edu/maps/middle_east_and_asia/mid-
dle_east98.jpg

Map of Khondab Atomic Weapons Facility

The Khondab atomic weapons facility is fairly new and generally hush-hush. The village of Khondab (aka Kondab or Kond Ab) is in the mountains at 5,859 feet above sea level, latitude 34" 6' 47N, longitude 51" 6' SE. It is about equally distant between Arak (lower right corner) and Hamadan (upper left border).

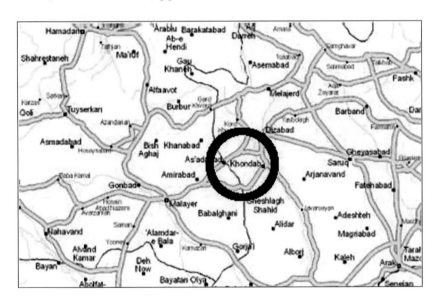

Map of Hinjan Atomic Weapons Facility

The Hinjan atomic weapons plant is top secret, but the town itself is on most good road maps. If you go to see it, do not have lunch at any place downwind from the plant.

Appendix B

Iran's Zoroastrian Teaching onGood and Evil

A human being can tell the difference between good and evil and can choose between them. This is a big responsibility for oneself and others. A person is good if he or she chooses to think good thoughts, speak good words, and do good deeds. A person is evil if he or she chooses to think evil thoughts, and that person will speak evil words and do evil deeds as well. Good deeds lead you to what is good, but evil deeds keep you away from it.

This implies...
- You can choose to think good thoughts.
- You can choose to speak good words.
- You can choose to do good deeds.
- You can choose to think evil thoughts.
- If you think evil thoughts, you will speak evil words and do evil deeds.
- You can't get to the good stuff by doing evil deeds, only by doing good deeds.
- Evil thoughts will prevent you from doing good deeds.
- You can change where you go by changing how you think.
- You can start right now.

Appendix C

President Bush's State of the Union Address 2002 First Mention of the Axis of Evil

Mr. Speaker, Vice President Cheney, members of Congress, distinguished guests, fellow citizens, as we gather tonight, our nation is at war, our economy is in a recession and the civilized world faces unprecedented dangers. Yet the state of our union has never been stronger.

We last met in an hour of shock and suffering. In four short months, our nation has comforted the victims, begun to rebuild New York and the Pentagon, rallied a great coalition, captured, arrested and rid the world of thousands of terrorists, destroyed Afghanistan's terrorist training camps, saved a people from starvation and freed a country from brutal oppression.

The American flag flies again over our embassy in Kabul. Terrorists who once occupied Afghanistan now occupy cells at Guantanamo Bay. And terrorist leaders who urged followers to sacrifice their lives are running for their own.

America and Afghanistan are now allies against terror. We will be partners in rebuilding that country. And this evening we welcome the distinguished interim leader of a liberated Afghanistan: Chairman Hamid Karzai.

The last time we met in this chamber, the mothers and daughters of Afghanistan were captives in their own homes, forbidden from working or going to school. Today women are free, and are part of Afghanistan's new government. And we welcome the new minister of women's affairs, Dr. Sima Samar.

Our progress is a tribute to the spirit of the Afghan people, to the resolve of our coalition and to the might of the United States military.

When I called our troops into action, I did so with complete confidence in their courage and skill. And tonight, thanks to them, we are winning the war on terror.

The men and women of our armed forces have delivered a message now clear to every enemy of the United States: Even 7,000 miles away, across oceans and continents, on mountaintops and in caves you will not escape the justice of this nation.

For many Americans, these four months have brought sorrow and pain that will never completely go away. Every day a retired firefighter returns to Ground Zero to feel closer to his two sons who died there. At a memorial in New York, a little boy left his football with a note for his lost father: "Dear Daddy, please take this to Heaven. I don't want to play football until I can play with you again someday." Last month, at the grave of her husband, Michael, a CIA officer and Marine who died in Mazar-e Sharif, Shannon Spann said these words of farewell: "Semper fi, my love." Shannon is with us tonight.

Shannon, I assure you and all who have lost a loved one that our cause is just, and our country will never forget the debt we owe Michael and all who gave their lives for freedom.

Our cause is just, and it continues. Our discoveries in Afghanistan confirmed our worst fears and showed us the true scope of the task ahead. We have seen the depth of our enemies' hatred in videos where they laugh about the loss of innocent life.

And the depth of their hatred is equaled by the madness of the destruction they design. We have found diagrams of American nuclear power plants and public water facilities, detailed instructions for making chemical weapons, surveillance maps of American cities, and thorough descriptions of landmarks in America and throughout the world.

What we have found in Afghanistan confirms that, far from ending there, our war against terror is only beginning. Most of the 19 men who hijacked planes on September the 11th were trained in Afghanistan's camps. And so were tens of thousands of others. Thousands of dangerous killers, schooled in the methods of murder, often supported by outlaw regimes, are now spread throughout the world like ticking time bombs, set to go off without warning.

Thanks to the work of our law enforcement officials and coalition partners, hundreds of terrorists have been arrested, yet tens of thousands of trained terrorists are still at large. These enemies view the entire world as a battlefield, and we must pursue them wherever they are. So long as training camps operate, so long as nations harbor terrorists, freedom is at risk and America and our allies must not, and will not, allow it.

Our nation will continue to be steadfast, and patient and persistent in the pursuit of two great objectives. First, we will shut down terrorist camps, disrupt terrorist plans and bring terrorists to justice. And second, we must prevent the terrorists and regimes who seek chemical, biological or nuclear weapons from threatening the United States and the world.

Our military has put the terror training camps of Afghanistan out of business, yet camps still exist in at least a dozen countries. A terrorist underworld — including groups like Hamas, Hezbollah, Islamic Jihad and Jaish-i-Mohammed — operates in remote jungles and deserts, and hides in the centers of large cities.

While the most visible military action is in Afghanistan, America is acting elsewhere. We now have troops in the Philippines helping to train that country's armed forces to go after terrorist cells that have executed an American and still hold hostages. Our soldiers, working with the Bosnian government, seized terrorists who were plotting to bomb our embassy. Our Navy is patrolling the coast of Africa to block the shipment of weapons and the establishment of terrorist camps in Somalia.

My hope is that all nations will heed our call and eliminate the terrorist parasites who threaten their countries and our own.

Many nations are acting forcefully. Pakistan is now cracking down on terror, and I admire the strong leadership of President Musharraf. But some governments will be timid in the face of terror. And make no mistake about it: If they do not act, America will.

Our second goal is to prevent regimes that sponsor terror from threatening America or our friends and allies with weapons of mass destruction.

Some of these regimes have been pretty quiet since September 11, but we know their true nature. North Korea is a regime arming with missiles and weapons of mass destruction, while starving its citizens.

Iran aggressively pursues these weapons and exports terror, while an unelected few repress the Iranian people's hope for freedom.

Iraq continues to flaunt its hostility toward America and to support terror. The Iraqi regime has plotted to develop anthrax and nerve gas and nuclear weapons for over a decade. This is a regime that has already used poison gas to murder thousands of its own citizens, leaving the bodies of mothers huddled over their dead children. This is a regime that agreed to international inspections then kicked out the inspectors. This is a regime that has something to hide from the civilized world.

States like these, and their terrorist allies, constitute an axis of evil, arming to threaten the peace of the world. By seeking weapons of mass destruction, these regimes pose a grave and growing danger. They could provide these arms to terrorists, giving them the means to match their hatred. They could attack our allies or attempt to blackmail the United States. In any of these cases, the price of indifference would be catastrophic.

We will work closely with our coalition to deny terrorists and their state sponsors the materials, technology and expertise to make and deliver weapons of mass destruction.

We will develop and deploy effective missile defenses to protect America and our allies from sudden attack.

And all nations should know: America will do what is necessary to ensure our nation's security.

We'll be deliberate, yet time is not on our side. I will not wait on events while dangers gather. I will not stand by as peril draws closer and closer. The United States of America will not permit the world's most dangerous regimes to threaten us with the world's most destructive weapons.

Our war on terror is well begun, but it is only begun. This campaign may not be finished on our watch, yet it must be and it will be waged on our watch.

We can't stop short. If we stopped now, leaving terror camps intact and terror states unchecked, our sense of security would be false and temporary. History has called America and our allies to action, and it is both our responsibility and our privilege to fight freedom's fight.

Our first priority must always be the security of our nation, and that will be reflected in the budget I send to Congress. My budget supports three great goals for America: We will win this war, we will protect our homeland, and we will revive our economy.

September 11 brought out the best in America and the best in this Congress, and I join the American people in applauding your unity and resolve. Now Americans deserve to have this same spirit directed toward addressing problems here at home.

I am a proud member of my party. Yet as we act to win the war, protect our people and create jobs in America, we must act first and foremost not as Republicans, not as Democrats, but as Americans.

It costs a lot to fight this war. We have spent more than a billion dollars a month — over $30 million a day — and we must be prepared for future operations. Afghanistan proved that expensive precision weapons defeat the enemy and spare innocent lives, and we need more of them. We need to replace aging aircraft and make our military more agile to put our troops anywhere in the world quickly and safely.

Our men and women in uniform deserve the best weapons, the best equipment and the best training and they also deserve another pay raise. My budget includes the largest increase in defense spending in two decades, because while the price of freedom and security is high, it is never too high. Whatever it costs to defend our country, we will pay.

The next priority of my budget is to do everything possible to protect our citizens and strengthen our nation against the ongoing threat of another attack.

Time and distance from the events of September the 11th will not make us safer unless we act on its lessons. America is no longer protected by vast oceans. We are protected from attack only by vigorous action abroad and increased vigilance at home.

My budget nearly doubles funding for a sustained strategy of homeland security, focused on four key areas: bioterrorism; emergency response; airport and border security; and improved intelligence.

We will develop vaccines to fight anthrax and other deadly diseases. We'll increase funding to help states and communities train and equip our heroic police and firefighters.

We will improve intelligence collection and sharing, expand patrols at our borders, strengthen the security of air travel, and use technology to track the arrivals and departures of visitors to the United States.

Homeland security will make America not only stronger but in many ways better. Knowledge gained from bioterrorism research will improve public health. Stronger police and fire departments will mean safer neighborhoods. Stricter border enforcement will help combat illegal drugs.

And as government works to better secure our homeland, America will continue to depend on the eyes and ears of alert citizens. A few days before Christmas, an airline flight attendant spotted a passenger lighting a match. The crew and passengers quickly subdued the man, who had been trained by al Qaeda and was armed with explosives. The people on that airplane were alert, and as a result likely saved nearly 200 lives. And tonight we welcome and thank flight attendants Hermis Moutardier and Christina Jones.

Once we have funded our national security and our homeland security, the final great priority of my budget is economic security for the American people. To achieve these great national objectives — to win the war, protect the homeland and revitalize our economy — our budget will run a deficit that will be small and short term so long as Congress restrains spending and acts in a fiscally responsible way.

Americans who have lost their jobs need our help, and I support extending unemployment benefits and direct assistance for health care coverage. Yet American workers want more than unemployment checks. They want a steady paycheck.

When America works, America prospers, so my economic security plan can be summed up in one word: jobs. Good jobs begin with good schools, and here we've made a fine start. Republicans and Democrats worked together to achieve historic education reform so that no child is left behind. I was proud to work with members of both parties, Chairman John Boehner and Congressman George Miller, Senator Judd Gregg. And I was so proud of our work I even had nice things to say about my friend Ted Kennedy.

There's more to do. We need to prepare our children to read and succeed in school with improved Head Start and early childhood development programs. We must upgrade our teacher colleges and teacher training and launch a major recruiting drive with a great goal for America: a quality teacher in every classroom.

Good jobs also depend on reliable and affordable energy. This Congress must act to encourage conservation, promote technology, build infrastructure, and it must act to increase energy production at home so America is less dependent on foreign oil.

Good jobs depend on expanded trade. Selling into new markets creates new jobs, so I ask Congress to finally approve trade promotion authority.

On these two key issues, trade and energy, the House of Representatives has acted to create jobs and I urge the Senate to pass this legislation.

Good jobs depend on sound tax policy. Last year, some in this hall thought my tax relief plan was too small, some thought it was too big. But when those checks arrived in the mail, most Americans thought tax relief was just about right.

Congress listened to the people and responded by reducing tax rates, doubling the child credit and ending the death tax. For the sake of long-term growth, and to help Americans plan for the future, let's make these tax cuts permanent.

The way out of this recession, the way to create jobs, is to grow the economy by encouraging investment in factories and equipment, and by speeding up tax relief so people have more money to spend. For the sake of American workers, let's pass a stimulus package. Good jobs must be the aim of welfare reform. As we reauthorize these important reforms, we must always remember: The goal is to reduce dependency on government and offer every American the dignity of a job.

Americans know economic security can vanish in an instant without health security. I ask Congress to join me this year to enact a Patients' Bill of Rights to give uninsured workers credits to help buy health coverage, to approve an historic increase in spending for veterans' health and to give seniors a sound and modern Medicare system that includes coverage for prescription drugs.

A good job should lead to security in retirement. I ask Congress to enact new safeguards for 401(k) and pension plans. Employees who have worked hard and saved all their lives should not have to risk losing everything if their company fails.

Through stricter accounting standards and tougher disclosure requirements, corporate America must be made more accountable to employees and shareholders and held to the highest standards of conduct.

Retirement security also depends upon keeping the commitments of Social Security, and we will. We must make Social Security financially stable and allow personal retirement accounts for younger workers who choose them.

Members, you and I will work together in the months ahead on other issues: productive farm policy, a cleaner environment, broader home ownership, especially among minorities and ways to encourage the good work of charities and faith-based groups.

I ask you to join me on these important domestic issues in the same spirit of cooperation we have applied to our war against terrorism.

During these last few months, I've been humbled and privileged to see the true character of this country in a time of testing. Our enemies believed America was weak and materialistic, that we would splinter in fear and selfishness. They were as wrong as they are evil. The American people have responded magnificently, with courage and compassion, strength and resolve. As I have met the heroes, hugged the families and looked into the tired faces of rescuers, I have stood in awe of the American people.

And I hope you will join me in expressing thanks to one American for the strength and calm and comfort she brings to our nation in crisis: our first lady, Laura Bush.

None of us would ever wish the evil that was done on September 11th, yet after America was attacked, it was as if our entire country looked into a mirror and saw our better selves. We were reminded that we are citizens, with obligations to each other, to our country and to history. We began to think less of the goods we can accumulate and more about the good we can do.

For too long our culture has said, "If it feels good, do it." Now America is embracing a new ethic and a new creed: "Let's roll." In the sacrifice of soldiers, the fierce brotherhood of firefighters, and the bravery and generosity of ordinary citizens, we have glimpsed what a new culture of responsibility could look like. We want to be a Nation that serves goals larger than self. We have been offered a unique opportunity, and we must not let this moment pass.

My call tonight is for every American to commit at least two years, 4,000 hours over the rest of your lifetime, to the service of your neighbors and your nation.

Many are already serving and I thank you. If you aren't sure how to help, I've got a good place to start. To sustain and extend the best that has emerged in America, I invite you to join the new USA Freedom Corps.

The Freedom Corps will focus on three areas of need: responding in case of crisis at home, rebuilding our communities, and extending American compassion throughout the world. One purpose of the USA Freedom Corps will be homeland security. America needs retired doctors and nurses who can be mobilized in major emergencies ... volunteers to help police and fire departments, transportation and utility workers well-trained in spotting danger.

Our country also needs citizens working to rebuild our communities. We need mentors to love children, especially children whose parents are in prison, and we need more talented teachers in troubled schools. USA Freedom Corps will expand and improve the good efforts of AmeriCorps and Senior Corps to recruit more than 200,000 new volunteers.

And America needs citizens to extend the compassion of our country to every part of the world. So we will renew the promise of the Peace Corps, double its volunteers over the next five years, and ask it to join a new effort to encourage development, and education, and opportunity in the Islamic world.

This time of adversity offers a unique moment of opportunity, a moment we must seize to change our culture. Through the gathering momentum of millions of acts of service and decency and kindness, I know: We can overcome evil with greater good.

And we have a great opportunity during this time of war to lead the world toward the values that will bring lasting peace. All fathers and mothers, in all societies, want their children to be educated and live free from poverty and violence. No people on Earth yearn to be oppressed, or aspire to servitude, or eagerly await the midnight knock of the secret police.

If anyone doubts this, let them look to Afghanistan, where the Islamic "street" greeted the fall of tyranny with song and celebration. Let the skeptics look to Islam's own rich history — with its centuries of learning, and tolerance, and progress.

America will lead by defending liberty and justice because they are right and true and unchanging for all people everywhere. No nation owns these aspirations, and no nation is exempt from them. We have no intention of imposing our culture — but America will always stand firm for the non-negotiable demands of human dignity: the rule of law ... limits on the power of the state ... respect for women ... private property ... free speech ... equal justice ... and religious tolerance.

America will take the side of brave men and women who advocate these values around the world — including the Islamic world — because we have a greater objective than eliminating threats and containing resentment. We seek a just and peaceful world beyond the war on terror.

In this moment of opportunity, a common danger is erasing old rivalries. America is working with Russia, China, and India in ways we never have before to achieve peace and prosperity. In every region, free markets and free trade and free societies are proving their power to lift lives. Together with friends and allies from Europe to Asia, from Africa to Latin America, we will demonstrate that the forces of terror cannot stop the momentum of freedom.

The last time I spoke here, I expressed the hope that life would return to normal. In some ways, it has. In others, it never will. Those of us who have lived through these challenging times have been changed by them. We've come to know truths that we will never question: Evil is real, and it must be opposed.

Beyond all differences of race or creed, we are one country, mourning together and facing danger together. Deep in the American character, there is honor, and it is stronger than cynicism. Many have discovered again that even in tragedy, especially in tragedy, God is near.

In a single instant, we realized that this will be a decisive decade in the history of liberty — that we have been called to a unique role in human events. Rarely has the world faced a choice more clear or consequential.

Our enemies send other people's children on missions of suicide and murder. They embrace tyranny and death as a cause and a creed. We stand for a different choice — made long ago, on the day of our founding. We affirm it again today. We choose freedom and the dignity of every life.

Steadfast in our purpose, we now press on. We have known freedom's price. We have shown freedom's power. And in this great conflict, my fellow Americans, we will see freedom's victory.

Thank you, thank you all, and may God bless.

Appendix D

Known Iranian Government Attacks Against the United States

The Iranian government was behind these attacks . . .			
Year	Description	Location	Agent
1979	Iranian Hostage Crisis	Iran	various
1980	Murder of Ali Tabatabai	Maryland	D. Belfield
1983	Bombing of U.S. Embassy	Beirut	Hezbollah
1983	Killing of 241 U.S. Marines	Lebanon	Hezbollah
1984	Bombing of U. S. Consulate	Beirut	Hezbollah
1984	Murder of CIA Station Chief William Buckley	Lebanon	Hezbollah
1985	Hijacking of TWA Flight 847 from Greece to Beirut	Lebanon	Hezbollah
1985	Murder of U.S. Navy diver Robert Stethem	Lebanon	Hezbollah
1996	Khobar Towers bombing	Saudi Arabia	Hezbollah
1998	Bombing of U.S. Embassy	Kenya	al Qaeda
1998	Bombing of U.S. Embassy	Tanzania	al Qaeda
2001	World Trade Center	New York	al Qaeda
2003	Five bombings in Casablanca	Morocco	al Qaeda
2003	Three bombings in Riyadh	Saudi Arabia	al Qaeda
2004	Attacks on U.S. soldiers	Iraq	M. al Sadr
2004	Attacks on U.S. soldiers	Iraq	al Qaeda
2004	Attacks on U.S. soldiers	Iraq	Pasdaran

Appendix E

The Human Rights Declaration of Cyrus the Great

I am Cyrus, King of Kings, Great King, Powerful King, King of Babylon, King of Sumer and Akkad, King of four countries, son of Kambujieh the Great King, King of Shahr Enshan, grandson of Cyrus the Great King from the eternal dynasty whose descendants are covered by the affection of Ahura Mazda and whose government is close to the hearts of the people.

When I entered Babylon with tranquility and friendship, I sat on the Throne at the Palace of Babylon Kings, among joy and happiness of all the people. Marduk (God of Babylonians) whose exaltation I always sought, turned the hearts of the noble people of Babylon towards me.

My Great Army moved peacefully inside the city of Babylon. I did not let any damage and harm be inflicted upon the people of this city and the land of Sumer and Akkad. The thought of internal affairs and religious places of Babylon shook my heart.

I commanded all people be free in worshiping their own God and atheists not harm them. I commanded none of houses of the people be destroyed and nobody deprive the inhabitants of the city from living means.

I commanded all the Temples of the cities of Babylon, Ashu, Shush, Akkad and all lands situated on the other side of Dejleh erected in old times and closed, to be opened. I returned all the Gods of those Temples to their respective places to be stationed there always. I also returned the Gods of Sumer and Akkad brought by Nebonid to Babylon and caused anger to their Palace called "Happiness of Heart".

All the Kings living in all countries of the world, from upper sea to lower sea, and Kings of the west who lived in tents brought their precious gifts to Babylon and presented to me.

I gathered the inhabitants of these places, rebuilt their houses that were destroyed and granted peace and tranquility to all.

The Great God was pleased with me and bestowed his blessings to me, Cyrus, and my Kambujieh and all my armies.

Terms Used

Iran

"Iran" and "Persia" are different names for the same country. It was called Persia until 1935, when the name was changed to Iran.

Iranian

"Iranian" and "Persian" mean the same thing: a citizen of Iran or something pertaining to that country (e.g., Persian rug, Persian culture). This book uses "Persia" and "Persian" for things and events before 1935 and "Iran" and "Iranian" for things and events after 1935.

Iranian government & Khomeini outlaw regime

Prior to 1979, Iran always had a king, called a Shah. In 1979, Ayatollah Ruhollah Khomeini took over and ruled as the Supreme Leader until his death in 1989. Since his death Iran has been ruled by a small group of clerics who all knew him. This book uses the terms "Iranian government" and "Khomeini outlaw regime" to refer to this group and the government they control.

Supreme Leader (veli-e faqih)

Khomeini's attempt to create an Islamic version of the Pope, combined with the powers of a king or dictator. Many clerics opposed the Supreme Leader concept as un-Islamic, and several ayatollahs are still under house arrest as a result. The sub-ayatollah opponents of the concept have generally been silenced through more violent means.

Ayatollah

The highest, most spiritual level of Shi'ite Moslem cleric. In theory these should all be kindly, loving men with no evil passions, such as greed, lust, envy, anger, sloth, pride, or gluttony.

Hojatolislam

The second highest, second most spiritual level of Shi'ite cleric. In theory they should be living proof of what terrific men Islam can produce.

Wife

The adult female spouse (nine years or older) of an adult male (15 years or older). This is the highest level of personal, moral, and spiritual evolution women can achieve in Khomeini's version of Islam.

Prostitute

Under Iranian law, a woman who engages in sex for money without obtaining a government license for a sigeh (temporary marriage). Men can have as many sigehs as they can afford, but women are limited to one at a time, followed by a two-month cooling off period. The resulting children are considered legitimate.

Key Players in Iranian Politics

Ayatollah Ruhollah Khomeini

The founder of the Khomeini outlaw regime. He came to power in 1979 after the Shah left Iran. He replaced the lifetime office of Shah (king) with the lifetime office of Veli-e-faqih (Supreme Leader). He was the first Supreme Leader until his death in 1989.

Ayatollah Ali Khamenei

The current Supreme Leader and one of the two most powerful men in the Khomeini outlaw regime today. He was only a Hojatolislam during Khomeini's reign, but they promoted him to Ayatollah so that he would qualify to become the second Supreme Leader. He receives 20% of the profits on all car sales in Iran, with the proceeds to be used for charitable purposes. Of course, nobody in Iran is more qualified than the Supreme Leader to decide what is or is not a charitable purpose. An Iranian defector has accused him of participating in the planning of 9/11 in a meeting with al Qaeda leaders in Tehran on May 4, 2001.

Ayatollah Ali Akbar Hashemi Rafsanjani

The President of Iran from 1989 to 1997 and one of the two most powerful men in the Khomeini outlaw regime today. He plays a major role in most important policy decisions, such as which overseas Iranians to murder and which missiles to buy. He is more skilled than Khamenei at appearing moderate, but their objectives are essentially the same: the destruction of Europe, Israel, and North America, the conquest of all oil-producing nations in the Middle East, and the eventual cultural conquest of the entire world. He has business experience, and his family would probably be listed on the Forbes 400 if the magazine was able to form a reliable estimate of their holdings, which include copper mining, television, pistachio exporting, oil, public construction projects, a Daewoo auto assembly plant, and an airline company. An Iranian defector has accused him of participating in the planning of 9/11 in a meeting with al Qaeda leaders in Tehran on May 4, 2001.

Hojatolislam Mohammad Khatami

The current president of Iran. He took office in 1997 and will be termed out in 2005. He has more public relations experience than anyone else in the Khomeini organization. He has successfully portrayed himself as a moderate. He supports the Khomeini agenda of destruction and world conquest, but he is willing to give women and college students a little more breathing room, as long as the power structure is not changed. He sometimes does a good cop/bad cop routine with the hardliners, in which the hardline agenda wins and he comes off as a nice guy who wants to do the right thing but just doesn't have the power. The routine fools some people in the West but very few people in Iran. Conditions have gotten steadily worse during his presidency. He has not been accused of involvement in 9/11 and is not believed to be involved in the Iranian government's decisions on whom to assassinate and when.

Ayatollah Ali Akbar Nateq-Nouri

A Khomeini outlaw regime hardiner. He ran against Khatami in the 1997 presidential election and after losing was appointed to head the Ministry of Information and Security, which is responsible for gathering intelligence information and planning terrorist operations worldwide. He is the reputed author of a memorandum dated May 14, 2001, that directs Ministry employees to think up joint terrorism projects for the Iranian government and al Qaeda. The memorandum also forbids them from contacting or dealing with any al Qaeda representatives except two specified individuals.

Ayatollah Ali Hussein Montazeri

A former Khomeini insider who was once expected to become the second Supreme Leader after Khomeini's death. He lost the job when he criticized the slaughter of more than 8,000 prisoners after the end of the Iraq-Iran War in 1988. He was stripped of all power and authority but allowed to keep his life, home, and wealth. He was placed under house arrest a few years later.

Ayatollah Ahmad Jannati

A member of the Council of Guardians and the leader of the Islamic Propagation Organization. He urged the Iraqi people to attack American soldiers shortly after the invasion of Iraq.

Ayatollah Ali Fallahian

A former director of the Ministry of Information and Security. He helped plan terrorist activities in Europe, including the 1992 Mykonos Restaurant killing in Berlin and the bombing of the Jewish community center in Buenos Aires in 1994. He was also the first Prosecutor for Khomeini's Special Court for the Clergy.

Ayatollah Kazem Shariatmadari

He opposed the Shah prior to 1979 but got into trouble with the Khomeini outlaw regime afterward, because he opposed the position of Supreme Leader. He was under house arrest from 1980 until his death in 1986. His supporters were not allowed to have a public funeral.

Ayatollah Hassan Tabataba'i-Qomi

He opposed the position of Supreme Leader. In 1985, he opposed continuing the war with Iraq and urged a settlement with Saddam Hussein. He was placed under house arrest in 1984 and has never been released from it.

Ayatollah Mohammed Sadeq Rouhani

He opposed the position of Supreme Leader and vigorously advocated for accountability in government and giving people the right to protest. He was placed under house arrest in 1985.

Ayatollah Mahdavi-Damaghani

He was arrested and tortured in the mid-1980s for opposing the government. The torture consisted of being punched and kicked by about 12 people, which is considered light torture by Khomeini outlaw regime standards. The incident is important because it shows clearly how much respect the Khomeini outlaw regime actually has for ayatollahs who are not Khomeini insiders: none.

Endnotes

1. A Crossfire War – Egypt after Nasser: Confronting Iran and the Jihad, www.iranmania.com/News/ArticleView/Default.asp?-NewsCode=26470 &NewsKind=Current%20Affairs
2. Also known as Zarathushtra or Zarathustra.
3. See Appendix B for a further discussion of good and evil in the Zoroastrian context.
4. W. Morgan Shuster, *The Strangling of Persia*, Century Co., 1912, introduction.
5. Qajar was the dynasty name, and Shah was his job title.
6. W. Morgan Shuster, *The Strangling of Persia*, The Century Co., 1912.
7. History of Iran: Pahlavi Dynasty, http://www.iranchamber.com/history/pahlavi/pahlavi.php.
8. Too Much, Too Fast... and too many mistakes. The Shah's budget director looks back, Harvard University Iranian Oral History Project, http:/www.iranian.com/History/Aug98/Madjidi/index.html.
9. A Crossfire War — Egypt after Nasser: Confronting Iran and the Jihad, www.iranmania.com/News/ArticleView/Default.asp?-NewsCode=26470&NewsKInd=Current%20Affairs
10. Monique Girgis, Islam's Appeal to Women: the Rise of Islamic Fundamentalism, http:/www.imaginary.com/~maen-ad/thesis/chapter2.html.
11. Lunch with Khomeini: How a Former SAVAK Chief Saved the Ayatollah's Life, Harvard Iranian Oral Studies Project, http:/www.iranian.com/History/Dec98/Pakravan.
12. Memoirs of Fatemeh Pakravan, Wife of General Hassan Pakravan, Harvard Iranian Oral History Project, http:/www.activistchat.com/iran.
13. Cyrus Kadivar, Dialogue of Murder, *Rouzegar-Now*, January 9, 2003
14. Cyrus Kadivar, Dialogue of Murder, *Rouzegar-Now*, January 9, 2003
15. Cyrus Kadivar, Dialogue of Murder, *Rouzegar-Now*, January 9, 2003
16. Borzou Daragahi, France Steps Up Its Investments in Iran, *New York Times*, June 23, 2004
17. Iran's Terrorism Abroad, www.ascfusa.org/publications/american_century/americancentury_madness_terrorism.htm
18. Cyrus Kadivar, Dialogue of Murder, *Rouzegar-Now*, January 9, 2003
19. http:/www.amnestyusa.org/regions/middleeast/document.do?id-=BC7ABDB06436BBB9802569A500714EF4.

20. 1999 Country Reports on Human Rights Practices, the Bureau of Democracy, Human Rights, and Labor, United States Department of State, February 25, 2000

21. Iran's Terrorism Abroad, http:/www.ascfusa.org/publications/american_century/americancentury_madness-_terrorism.htm

22. Khatami's Big - and Possibly - Irreparable Blunder, Iran Press Service, http:/www.iran-press-service.com/articles/lajevardi.html.

23. Human Rights Watch Condemns Detention of an Iranian Dissident, http:/hrw.org/press98/sept/iran909.htm.

24. Islamic Republic's torturers and their torture masters, http:/www.iricrimes.org/wanted.asp.

25. Canadian arrested in Iran brain dead after beating: family, CBC News, July 11, 2003

26. Iran Says Canadian Journalist Died from Beatings, Reuters, July 16, 2003.

27. Iran appoints veteran judge to investigate Iranian-Canadian photojournalist's death *San Francisco Chronicle*, July 25, 2003.

28. Brian Whitaker, Lawyer to pursue Iran jail killer, *The Guardian*, July 26, 2004

29. The 2004 oil shortage is presently attributed to dwindling oil supplies in the existing oil fields combined with increased demand in China for both industrial and consumer uses and increased demand in the United States based on such factors as the war in Iraq, the popularity of sports utility vehicles, and the unwillingness of oil companies to attempt to build new refineries against the opposition of environmental activists.

30. Call for European Union to Break with Iran Over Journalist's Death, http:/www.iranvajahan.net/cgi-bin/news_en.pl?l=en&y=2003&m=07&d=26&a=6

31. Ali Akbar Dareini, Iran appoints veteran judge to investigate Iranian-Canadian photojournalist's death, *San Francisco Chronicle*, Friday, July 25, 2003

32. Iran halts journalist death trial, *The Guardian* (UK), July 19, 2004

33. Brian Whitaker, Lawyer to pursue Iran jail killer, *The Guardian*, July 26, 2004

34. Alcohol-based medicines were originally invented in Persia.

35. All examples taken from Monitoring Human Rights In Iran, www.iricrimes.org/local_s_0304.asp.

36. Iran's hardliners 'crush dissent with torture', *The Guardian*, June 7, 2004

37.   Human Rights and Terrorism, Access to Medication, Rights to Food, Health among Issues, United Nations Press Release No. GA/10223, December 22, 2003

38.   Amnesty International Annual Report 2004, Iran

39.   Ali Akbar Dareini, Iran Frees Academic Who Was Twice Condemned to Death for Blasphemy, Associated Press, July 31, 2004

40.   Ali Akbar Dareini, Iran Frees Academic Who Was Twice Condemned to Death for Blasphemy, Associated Press, July 31, 2004

41.   Ali Akbar Dareini, Iran Frees Academic Who Was Twice Condemned to Death for Blasphemy, Associated Press, July 31, 2004

42.   Ali Akbar Dareini, Iran Frees Academic Who Was Twice Condemned to Death for Blasphemy, Associated Press, July 31, 2004

43.   VOA Producer's Father Murdered in Iran, www.iran.org/tib/public/5202.htm

44.   The Trials of Everyday Life, *The Economist,* January 18, 2003

45.   World's Toughest Underwear Sale, Reuters, August 31, 2004

46.   World's Toughest Underwear Sale, Reuters, August 31, 2004

47.   The Trials of Everyday Life, *The Economist* January 18, 2003

48.   Young men and women sentenced to beatings, Reuters, March, 2000

49.   People convicted more than once of owning a satellite dish can be sent to prison for up six years, under a 1994 law passed by the Majlis. Final Report on the situation of human rights in the Islamic Republic of Iran by the Special Representative of the UN Commission on Human Rights.

50.   On 12 August 1994, nine women were arrested in a private home in the Karim-Khan-e-Zand district in the north of Tehran for playing cards., Final Report on the situation of human rights in the Islamic Republic of Iran by the Special Representative of the UN Commission on Human Rights.

51.   The Trials of Everyday Life, *The Economist* January 18, 2003

52.   The neighboring country of Afghanistan produces enormous quantities of opium, heroin, morphine, and hashish.

53.   The Curse of Westoxification, *The Economist,* January 187, 2003

54.   The Curse of Westoxification, *The Economist,* January 187, 2003

55.   The Curse of Westoxification, *The Economist*, January 18, 2003.

56.   Michael Rubin, The will of the Iranian people should not be ignored this time around, *National Review*, July 26, 2002.

57.   Michael Rubin, The will of the Iranian people should not be ignored this time around, *National Review*, July 26, 2002.

58.   Iran Stones Six to Death, Associated Press, October 26, 1997

59. Factbook on Global Sexual Exploitation— Iran, www.uri.edu/artsci/wms/hughes/iran.htm.
60. Court in Iran sentences prostitution ring members to over 4,000 lashes, www.corpun.com/irj00301.htm.
61. The Curse of Westoxification, *The Economist*, January 18, 2003.
62. Monique Girgis, Women in Post-Revolutionary Iran, www.imaginary.com/~maenad/thesis/chapter3.html.
63. Monique Girgis, Women in Post-Revolutionary Iran, www.imaginary.com/~maenad/thesis/chapter3.html.
64. Javaad Zargooshi, M.D., Characteristics of gonorrhoea in Kermanshah, Iran, http:/sextrans.bmjjournals.com/cgi/content/abstract/78/6/460
65. Javaad Zargooshi, M.D., Characteristics of gonorrhoea in Kermanshah, Iran, http:/sextrans.bmjjournals.com/cgi/content/abstract/78/6/460
66. Jean Shaoul, Eyewitness in Iran: Bam disaster threatens to ignite political powder keg, January 14, 2004, www.wsws.org/articles/2004/jan2004/iran-j14.shtml.
67. One Million Street-children in Iran, www.iraniancivilrights.com/streetchildren.htm.
68. More than 35% of street children addicted to drugs, *Khorassan Daily*, February 29, 2004
69. Tehran opens home for street children, www.iran-e-sabz.org/news/youth7.htm.
70. Trafficking Gangs Rent Street Children for 125 United States Dollars per Year, *Etemad Daily*, March 7, 2004
71. 23,000 Street Children Gathered in Tehran, *Hamshahri Daily*, March 17, 2004
72. 150 children end up in Iran courts daily for harassment: Daily, *Hayat-e No Daily*, November 20, 2001
73. Mehrnoosh Pourziai, A Report on the Condition of Young Children in Rug-Weaving Sweatshops, [English Translation by Zarin Shaghaghi], www.iranianchildren.org/rugsweat.html
74. Mehrnoosh Pourziai, A Report on the Condition of Young Children in Rug-Weaving Sweatshops, [English Translation by Zarin Shaghaghi], www.iranianchildren.org/rugsweat.html
75. Maryam Bijani, The High Cost of Child Labor, [English Translation by Zarin Shaghaghi], Sedaye Edalat, www.iranianchildren.org/childlabor_02.html.

76. Maryam Bijani, The High Cost of Child Labor, [English Translation by Zarin Shaghaghi], Sedaye Edalat, www.iranianchildren.org/childlabor_02.html.

77. Shirin Ebadi, Conviction Of The Children Under The Laws Of The 76 Years Ago Is Better Than The Current Laws,[English Translation by Zarin Shaghaghi], www.iranianchildren.org/ebadiconviction.html

78. Shirin Ebadi, Conviction Of The Children Under The Laws Of The 76 Years Ago Is Better Than The Current Laws,[English Translation by Zarin Shaghaghi], www.iranianchildren.org/ebadiconviction.html

79. Shirin Ebadi, Conviction Of The Children Under The Laws Of The 76 Years Ago Is Better Than The Current Laws,[English Translation by Zarin Shaghaghi], www.iranianchildren.org/ebadiconviction.html

80. Under current Iranian law, criminal defendants are entitled to an attorney even if they cannot afford one.

81. The stories vary on whether it was merely a scarf or something more.

82. Girl, 16, Hanged in Public in Iran, www.iranfocus.com/modules/news/article.php?storyid=80.

83. Alasdair Palmer, Death and the Maiden in Iran, *The Telegraph,* August 29, 2004

84. The Heartbreaking and Enraging Story of a 16 year old girl's execution past Sunday in the Town of Neka, www.activistchat.com/phpBB2/viewtopic.php?t=3661&highlight=.

85. Mullahs Commit another Heinous Crime, www.iranvajahan.net/cgi-bin/news.pl?l=en&y=2—4&d=27&a=6.

86. Amnesty International Outraged at Execution of a 16 year old girl, Amnesty International Public Statement, August 23, 2004

87. Parvin Darabi, My Testimony, Why I am not a Muslim, www.faithfreedom.org/Testimonials/parvin.htm.

88. Parvin Darabi, My Testimony, Why I am not a Muslim, www.faithfreedom.org/Testimonials/parvin.htm.

89. Parvin Darabi, My Testimony, Why I am not a Muslim, www.faithfreedom.org/Testimonials/parvin.htm.

90. Ayatollah & Women, The Eyeranian, September 15, 2003, www.eyeranian.net/2003/09/15,348.shtml.

91. Ayatollah & Women, The Eyeranian, September 15, 2003, www.eyeranian.net/2003/09/15,348.shtml.

92. Report of the Special Representative of the Commission of Human Rights of the United Nations in the Islamic Republic of Iran, 1992, www.faithfreedom.org/Testimonials/parvin.htm.

93. Message to the Congress of the United States, Office of the White House Press Secretary, November 12, 2003

94. Executive Order 12957.

95. Notice: Continuation of the National Emergency with Respect to Iran, White House Press Release, March 10, 2004

96. The term atomic bomb dates back to the 1940s and is less common today than the term nuclear weapons. This book uses both terms. The term atomic bomb helps remind us what these weapons actually do.

97. http:/www.president.ir/khatami/khbio-e.htm

98. Khatami Involved in 1988 Massacre of Political Prisoners, *Sunday Telegraph*, February 4, 2001

99. Khatami, Moderate or Terrorist?, voiceofiran.com/catalog.html

100. Kenneth R. Timmerman, Evidence Fuels Iran Terror Debate, *Insight*, June 10, 2003.

101. Iran Promises 'Strong Action' Over Envoy's Arrest, Reuters, August 24, 2003

102. Iran Promises 'Strong Action' Over Envoy's Arrest, Reuters, August 24, 2003

103. Iran Promises 'Strong Action' Over Envoy's Arrest, Reuters, August 24, 2003

104. Amir Taheri, The Mullah's Shock, *New York Post*, September 8, 2003.

105. Amir Taheri, The Mullah's Shock, *New York Post*, September 8, 2003.

106. Louis Freeh's final act, Daniel Schorr, Christian Science Monitor, May 11, 2001

107. Freeh: I Turned to Bush After Clinton Blocked Khobar Terror Probe, www.newsmax.com/showinside.shtml?a=2003/5/20/93708; Bush aide attacks Iran terror link: The US claims Iran was involved in the Khobar attack, BBC News, December 20, 2001

108. Bush aide attacks Iran terror link: The US claims Iran was involved in the Khobar attack, BBC News, December 20, 2001

109. Louis Freeh praises Saudi cooperation on Khobar investigation, Royal Embassy of Saudi Arabia, Press release, October 9, 2004

110. Adam Zagorin and Joe Klein, 9/11 Commission Finds Ties Between al-Qaeda and Iran, *Time*, July 16, 2004, www.time.com/time/nation/article/0,8599,664967,00.html

111. Judge rules Iran behind Marine barracks bombing, *Washington Post*, May 31, 2003.

112. Kenneth Timmerman, Lebanese Madman Leaves Trail of Terror, *VFW Magazine*, April, 2002

113. Kenneth R. Timmerman, Lebanese Madman Leaves Trail of TERROR, *VFW Magazine,* April, 2002

114. Kenneth Timmerman, Lebanese Madman Leaves Trail of Terror, *VFW Magazine*, April, 2002

115. Mr. Baer was an exceptionally talented CIA case officer who successfully recruited an astonishing number of Arabic and Iranian informants. Unfortunately, his reports and comments were often ignored or not acted upon by Washington. It is particularly distressing to think that the Beirut embassy bombing might have been prevented if the reports of Mr. Baer and other CIA officers had been heeded.

116. Robert Baer, *See No Evil,* Crown Publishers, New York, 2002.

117. As of the writing of this book, Khatami's presidency has a few more months to go. However, the likelihood of Iran mounting a more spectacular terrorist attack during that time is minimal, with over 100,000 American army troops located next door in Iraq.

118. Statement of Larry A. Mefford to the United States Senate Terrorism, Technology and Homeland Security Subcommittee, Washington, D.C. on June 27, 2003

119. An Iranian-French agent of the Iranian government wrote a book claiming that the 9/11 attacks were planned and carried out by Israel and the United States. When asked why Osama bin Laden claimed credit for the attacks, he claimed that Osama was an American agent. His book sold over 100,000 copies in Europe.

120. Joseph Farah, Iran Supporting al-Qaida Terror, World Net Daily, November 8, 2004.

121. Adam Zagorin and Joe Klein, 9/11 Commission Finds Ties Between al-Qaeda and Iran, *Time*, July 16, 2004, www.time.com/time/nation/article/0,8599,664967,00.html

122. Kenneth R. Timmerman, Iran Cosponsors Al-Qaeda Terrorism, *Insight,* Nov. 9, 2001.

123. Adam Zagoria & Joe Klein, 9/11 Commission Finds Ties Between al-Qaeda and Iran, *Time*, July 16, 2004

124. Kenneth Timmerman, Defector Alleged Iranian Involvement in Sept. 11 Attacks, *Insight*, June 10, 2003

125. Kenneth Timmerman, Defector Alleged Iranian Involvement in Sept. 11 Attacks, *Insight*, June 10, 2003

126. Some readers may wonder why Zakeri believes the final plan was developed on May 4th, when the memo of May 14th says Iran and al Qaeda need to find one objective. The most likely explanation is that the memo

is intentionally false, so that anyone reading it would believe Iran was not involved in the planning of 9/11 as of May, 2001. People who did not know about the meeting on May 4, 2001, could easily be deceived in this way. This type of deceitfulness is common among Khomeini outlaw regime insiders.

127. John Credson and Cam Simpson, Surprise Witness Delays Verdict in Sept. 11 Trial in Germany, Chicago Tribune, January 21, 2004

128. Kenneth R. Timmerman, Defector Points Finger at Iran in September 11 plot, Insight on the News, February 4, 2004.

129. German Court Acquits 9/11 Terror Suspect, Associated Press, February 5, 2004

130. Joseph Farah, Iran Supporting al-Qaida Terror, World Net Daily, November 8, 2004.

131. Crashed Military Plane was an Ilyushin-76, www.iranmania.com/News/ArticleView/Default.asp?ArchiveNews=Yes

132. Ilyushin Crash Puts Spotlight Back on Perils of Iran's Skies, www.iranmania.com/News/ArticleView/Default.asp?NewsCode=14384

133. Joseph Farah, Iran Supporting al-Qaida Terror, World Net Daily, November 8, 2004.

134. Rowan Scarborough, Iran, Hezbollah support al-Sadr, *Washington Times,* April 7, 2004

135. Mahan Abedin, The Sadrist Movement, *Middle East Intelligence Bulletin*, July, 2003

136. Paul Sullivan, Sistani, Sadr, and the Shia: The Whole World is Watching, *History News Network,* http://hnn.us/articles/4975.htmlhttp://hnn.us/articles/4975.html

137. Mahan Abedin, The Sadrist Movement, *Middle East Intelligence Bulletin*, July, 2003

138. Julie Stahl, Iran Fighting Proxy War Against United States Through Iraqi Shiites, Hizballah, www.crosswalk.com/news/1279178.html

139. Khomeini's network of spies in Tehran in November of 1979 was so vast and thorough that it is virtually certain that someone in the Khomeini government knew about the student conspiracy. It is almost inconceivable that they would keep Khomeini in the dark about it. It is far more likely that either Khomeini people planned it or let it proceed without interference to see what would happen.

140. Apparently not related to Sadegh Tabatabai, Khomeini's son in law.

141. Final Report on the Situation of Human Rights in the Islamic Republic of Iran, http://www.iricrimes.org/lr_int.asp?pgn=bakhtiar.

142. Josh Gerstein, Silver Screen Assassin: Admitted Killer's Role in Kandahar Film Outrages Victim's Family, ABC News, December 29, 2003.

143. Murder of the Foruhars Carried Out by the Secret Operations Committee, http://www.iran-press-service.com/articles/5dariush_parveneh.html

144. Robert H. Ferrell, *The American Secretaries of State and Their Diplomacy: Vol. XV, George C. Marshall,* Cooper Square, New York, 1966, pp. 230-231.

145. The remainder of his service was spent aboard a naval ship too far off the Vietnamese coast for the enemy forces to reach.

146. South Africa gave up its nuclear weapons shortly before allowing Nelson Mandela to run for president, and three of the former Soviet Socialist Republics gave all their nuclear weapons to Russia after the breakup of the Soviet Union.

147. Iran, China Conclude $4.5 Billion Arms Deal, *Washington Post*, October 3, 1996

148. Lt. Gen. Michael DeLong, *Inside Centcom*, Regnery, 2004, p. 135.

149. Michael Eisenstadt, Russian Arms and Technology Transfers to Iran: Policy Challenges for the United States, *Arms Control Today*, March 2001

150. Matthew Rice, Clinton Signs 'Iran Nonproliferation Act' , *Arms Control Today,* April 2000

151. Press briefing by White House Press Secretary Ari Fleischer, March 10, 2003

152. Carl Weiser and Patrick Jackson, Iranian-American Fund-raiser Sparks Political Spat in Delaware, March 28, 2002

153. Kenneth R. Timmerman, Biden Buddies Up to Pro-Iran Lobby, *Insight on the News*, April 15, 2002

154. Senator Biden Urges Caution on Iran, Associated Press, May 27, 2003

155. Senator Biden Urges Caution on Iran, Associated Press, May 27, 2003

156. Senior United States Senator Biden Meets Iranian FM Kamal Kharrazi in Davos, www.payk.net/mailingLists/iran-news/html/current/msg00225.html,

157. George Perkovich, How to defuse the Iranian bomb, *Asian Age*, June 16, 2003

158. Andrew Koch & Alon Ben-David, Iran's nuclear work revealed, *Janes*, June 24, 2003

159. Michael Eisenstadt, Iran's Nuclear Program: Gathering Dust or Gaining Steam? Washington Institute for Near East Policy, February 3, 2003

160. Implementation of the NPT safeguards agreement in the Islamic Republic of Iran Report by the Director General, International Atomic Energy Agency, June 6, 2003

161. Iran: Stuck On The Axis Of Evil? *The Economist*, January 20, 2003

162. Ian Traynor and Dan De Luce, UN watchdog presses Iran on nuclear inspections, *The Guardian*, June 16, 2003

163. Speech by John S. Wolf, US Assistant Secretary of State for Non-Proliferation, to the Monterey Institute Non-Proliferation Strategy Group, Stockholm, Sweden, September 6, 2002

164. Rafsanjani Says Muslims Should Use Nuclear Weapon Against Israel (Iran), Iran Press Service, March 12, 2003

165. This analysis assumes that the Iranian government actually suspended uranium enrichment and is not simply lying. If it turns out they were lying, what can the Europeans do about it? The French and Germans have already said that they would not invade Iran under any circumstances.

166. Why We Fight America: Al-Qaida Spokesman Explains September 11 and Declares Intentions to Kill 4 Million Americans with Weapons of Mass Destruction, The Middle East Media Research Institute, June 21, 2002

167. The World Trade Center attack killed slightly under 3,000 people and cost al Qaeda an estimated $500,000 to plan and carry out. At that rate, staggering as it is, it would take 1,334 more attacks at a cost of over $666,000,000 to reach the four million mark. By making areas of land too radioactive to inhabit, nuclear weapons would also advance al Qaeda more quickly toward their goal of eight million homeless Americans.

168. William Robert Johnston, Osama bin Laden and nuclear weapons, http://www.johnstonsarchive.net/nuclear/osamanuk.html.

169. William Robert Johnston, Osama bin Laden and nuclear weapons, http://www.johnstonsarchive.net/nuclear/osamanuk.html.

170. Robert Jaques, UK workers beheaded on Bin Laden's orders: Terror king paid kidnappers $30m blood money to murder telco engineers, http://www.vnunet.com/news/1126991.

171. Iran Delivered Missiles to Hezbollah in Lebanon via Syria, Middle East Research Institute, August 19, 2004

172. Hezbollah Re-Elects Sheik Hassan Nasrallah As Leader for Fifth Term, Associated Press, August 17, 2004

173. Edward T. Pound, The Iran Connection, *U.S. News & World Report*, November 22, 2004.

174. An Open Letter: The Hizballah Program, *Jerusalem Quarterly*, Fall 1988 [abridged translation of Nass al-Risala al-Maftuha allati wajahaha Hizballah ila-l-Mustad'afin fi Lubnan wa-l-Alam, al-Safir (Beirut), February 16, 1985]
175. Iran Approves Uranium Enrichment, CNN, October 31, 2004.
176. Majlis Approves Bill on Access to Civilian Nuclear Technology, Tehran Times, October 31, 2004
177. John Gibson, *Hating America* (HarperCollins 2004), p. 74.
178. Ayelet Savyon, The Internal Debate in Iran: How to Respond to Western Pressure Regarding Its Nuclear Programs, http://www.memri.org/bin/articles.cgi?Area=iran&ID=IA18104
179. Ayelet Savyon, The Internal Debate in Iran: How to Respond to Western Pressure Regarding Its Nuclear Programs, http://www.memri.org/bin/articles.cgi?Area=iran&ID=IA18104
180. Nasser Karimi, 200 Pledge Willingness to Carry Out Suicide Attacks Against Americans, CBC News, December 3, 2004.
181. Nasser Karimi, 200 Pledge Willingness to Carry Out Suicide Attacks Against Americans, CBC News, December 3, 2004.
182. Nasser Karimi, 200 Pledge Willingness to Carry Out Suicide Attacks Against Americans, CBC News, December 3, 2004.
183. Iran Threatens the United States and the West, http://www.freemuslims.org/news/article.php?article=65
184. IAEA Seeks Access to Suspect Iran Military Sites, www.iranmania.com, December 2, 2004.
185. Iran Backs Out from Threat to State Anti-United States Preemptive Strikes, August 22, 2004, www.naharnet.com/dom-ino/tn/NewsDesk.nsf/story/587C9EF97809B06C2256EF7002DA
186. Stephen E. Ambrose, *Eisenhower: Soldier and President,* Touchstone, New York, 3rd ed., 1990, pp. 285-286.
187. Iranian Missile Can Reach Israel, Associated Press, July 4, 2003
188. Ayelet Savyon, The Internal Debate in Iran: How to Respond to Western Pressure Regarding Its Nuclear Programs, http://www.memri.org/bin/articles.cgi?Area=iran&ID=IA18104
189. IAEA Seeks Access to Suspect Iran Military Sites, www.iranmania.com, December 2, 2004.
190. Rafsanjani Says Muslims Should Use Nuclear Weapon Against Israel, Iran Press Service, December 14, 2001
191. Amir Oren, Iran's successful missile test puts Israel within range; United States is `gravely concerned' by Shihab-3 ground-to-ground rocket, Haaretz, July 04, 2003
192. North Korea Exports Missiles to Iran by Air, Kyodo News Service, June 15, 2003

193. 1999 Final Report of the North Korea Advisory Group to The Speaker of the United States House of Representatives, November, 1999

194. This book advocates that the taking should be done by the Iranian people, with the aid and support of the United States and the Iranian-American community.

195. The United States, as a nation, is less than 250 years old.

196. Dean Acheson, *Present at the Creation: My Years at the State Department* (Norton, 1969), pp. 197-198.

197. Developments in the Azerbaijan Situation, Central Intelligence Group Office of Reports and Estimates, declassified Secret memo, June 4, 1947. The Central Intelligence Group was a precursor to the Central Intelligence Agency.

198. The containment doctrine held that the United States should prevent the Soviet Union and other Communist countries from expanding, by entering into alliances with countries that they might otherwise turn to Communism. It worked for about 20 years, until our alliance with South Vietnam failed to contain the expansion of North Vietnam.

199. Ali M. Ansari, *Modern Iran Since 1921: The Pahlavis and After* (London: Longman, 2003), p. 179.

200. Mossadegh's imperious attitude probably came in part from his family's high ranking in the aristocracy and long association with the Qajari dynasty. In 1925, Mossadegh was one of only four members of the Majlis to vote against replacing the Qajari dynasty with the Pahlavi dynasty in the person of Reza I.

201. During the Suez crisis in 1956 he supported Egypt's rights of national sovereignty over the Suez Canal and prevented Britain, France, and Israel from taking it away from Egypt.

202. Rich Hampson, United States Captives in Tehran Got First Taste of Terror, USA Today, October 25, 2004.

203. Rich Hampson, United States Captives in Tehran Got First Taste of Terror, USA Today, October 25, 2004.

204. This outcome was tragic but far preferable to having American soldiers captured in Tehran trying to find and rescue the hostages. The shortage of reliable information made this risk a significant possibility.

205. The Islamic Jihad ostensibly kidnaped him, but this is generally considered a fictitious business name for Hezbollah and the Iranian government, not a separate group of terrorists.

206. State of the Union Address, January 29, 2002.

207. Reza Pahlavi, *Winds of Change: the Future of Democracy in Iran*, Regnery, 2002, p. 61

208. Testimony of Steven Emerson before the Senate Foreign Relations Subcommittee on Near East and South Asian Affairs, May 14, 1998

209. Iranian Media Back Riyadh in its War of Words with Washington, Iran Press Service, August 22, 2002

210. Reza Pahlavi, *Winds of Change: the Future of Democracy in Iran*, Regnery, 2002, p. 56.

211. Reza Pahlavi, *Winds of Change: the Future of Democracy in Iran*, Regnery, 2002, p. 50.

212. In 1991 Iran purchased 1,000 kilograms [1.1 tons/2,204 pounds] of natural uranium hexafluoride, 400 kilograms [881 pounds] of uranium tetrafluoride, and 400 kilograms [881 pounds] of uranium dioxide from China. *Iran, player or rogue? The deadline is now. Will Iran come clean about its nuclear doings?*, David Albright & Corey Hinderstein, *Bulletin of the Atomic Scientists*, September/October 2003, Volume 59, No. 5, pp. 52c58

213. North Korea Plans to Export Missiles to Iran, Reuters, August 5, 2003.

214. Michael Eisenstadt, Russian Arms and Technology Transfers to Iran: Policy Challenges for the United States, *Arms Control Today*, March 2001

215. Reza Pahlavi, *Winds of Change: the Future of Democracy in Iran*, Regnery, 2002, p. 49.

216. Iran Runs Out of Cash to Import Petrol, Agence France-Presse, August 26, 2004

217. Iran, China Sign Biggest Energy Deal, Tehran Times, October 30, 2004

218. China Lacks Technology to Develop Yadavaran: expert, Tehran Times, November 1, 2004.

219. Paul Klebnikov, Millionaire Mullahs, http:/www.Iran va-Jahan.com

220. Iran Leader Denies Profiteering, BBC News, http:/new.bbc.co.uk/2/hi/middle_east/3068805.stm

221. Faramarz Nateghian, Industrial Challenges Facing Iran in the Third Millenium, *Andisheh*, March, 2001

222. Faramarz Nateghian, Industrial Challenges Facing Iran in the Third Millenium, *Andisheh*, March, 2001

223. Khatami outlines next Iran five-year plan, still dependent on oil, Agence France Presse, August 19, 1999

224. Hossein Derakhshan, Iran: Chinese or North Korean Style of Ruling, August 28, 2004, www.hoder.com/weblog.

225. The Communist Five Year Plans were most likely inspired by the Seven Year Plans of Czar Peter I (Peter the Great). His Seven Year Plans worked well and enabled Russia to narrow the economic and technological gaps with western Europe

226. Albrecht Frischenschlager, How Iran Finances Itself: An Analysis, http://www.mestrategies.com/finances_content.htm

227. South Korean, Japanese, French, and British, all respond to Iran for sale by mullahs, http://www.iranian.ws/iran_news/publish/article_2266.shtml

228. South Korean, Japanese, French, and British, all respond to Iran for sale by mullahs, http://www.iranian.ws/iran_news/publish/article_2266.shtml

229. Persian Carpet Exports Hit $600m, http://www.iranian.ws/iran_news/publish/article_3442.shtml.

230. Bruce Tober, Iran's telecoms: success amid sanctions, United Press International, April 11, 2002

231. Bruce Tober, Iran's telecoms: success amid sanctions, United Press International, April 11, 2002

232. Hossein Derakhshan, Physically Removing Web Servers, August 23, 2004

233. Human Rights Watch Slams Mullahs, Iran, December 6, 2004, www.iranian.ws/iran_news/publish/article_479.shtml

234. Reza Pahlavi, *Winds of Change: the Future of Democracy in Iran*, Regnery, 2002, p. 19.

235. Iran Faces Unusual Force: Pro-American Demonstrators, *Wall Street Journal*, November 5, 2001

236. Meeting with the President and CEO of NGS, www.rezapahlavi.org

237. William J. O'Neil, *The Successful Investor*, McGraw-Hill, 2004, p. 20.

238. Mohammad Mehdi Khorrami, Iranians in the United States www.pbs.org/visavis/BTVPages/Iranians_in_us.html.

239. The Persian Diaspora, www.farsinet.com/pwo/diaspora.html.

240. Nassim Nicholas Taleb, *Fooled by Randomness*, Texere, 2001, p. 20.

241. Khamenei banned them because he thought it was too exciting for men to see a woman in a chadoor riding a bicycle.

242. The Zoroastrian, Christian, and Jewish seats in the Majlis were not a Khomeini innovation but rather an Iranian tradition begun roughly 100 years ago by Ayatollah Behbahani and Jamshid Jamshidian, an influential Persian banker and the first Zoroastrian member of the Majlis.

243. Iran Seizes 2,000 Protestors, satellite dishes, as unrest spreads, *World Tribune*, October 28, 2001

244. Safa Haeri, The Hate of the People Reaching Explosion Point, http://www.iran-press-service.com/ips/articles-2004/september/iran_demos_28904.shtml.

245. Pro-Democracy Protest in Iran Gains Momentum, Reuters, September 27, 2004, www.alertnet.org/thenews/newsdesk/109627385730.htm.

246. Safa Haeri, The Hate of the People Reaching Explosion Point, http://www.iran-press-service.com/ips/articles-2004/september/iran_demos_28904.shtml.

247. Safa Haeri, The Hate of the People Reaching Explosion Point, http://www.iran-press-service.com/ips/articles-2004/september/iran_demos_28904.shtml.

248. Safa Haeri, The Hate of the People Reaching Explosion Point, http://www.iran-press-service.com/ips/articles-2004/september/iran_demos_28904.shtml.

249. Afsane Bassir-Pour, Iranian Regime Worried by People's Pro-Americanism Iran Press Service, April 27, 2003.

250. Afsane Bassir-Pour, Iranian Regime Worried by People's Pro-Americanism Iran Press Service, April 27, 2003.

251. Bibles are particularly dangerous to possess in Iran, because converting a Moslem to Christianity carries a death sentence.

252. Leslie Fulbright, Local Iranians Back United States Stand Against Saddam, *Seattle Times*, Jnaury 6, 2003.

253. United States government statistics support this argument. The Statistical Abstract of the United States for 2002 indicates that as of 2001, Iran had about 10,870,000 people fit to serve in the military. Pakistan had twice as many, Russia had 2.8 times as many, India had 15 times as many, and China had 18.4 times as many. Iraq and Israel had fewer people fit for military service, but in 2001 both those countries were suspected of having nuclear weapons.

254. Michael Ledeen, Iran's Next Revolution, *Wall Street Journal*, June 5, 2002.

255. W. Morgan Shuster, *The Strangling of Persia* (Century, 1912), pp. 241-242.

256. W. Morgan Shuster, *The Strangling of Persia* (Century, 1912), pp. 241-242.